Charles H. Tyndall

Object Sermons in Outline

With numerous illustrations

Charles H. Tyndall

Object Sermons in Outline
With numerous illustrations

ISBN/EAN: 9783337114510

Printed in Europe, USA, Canada, Australia, Japan

Cover: Foto ©Lupo / pixelio.de

More available books at **www.hansebooks.com**

OBJECT SERMONS

IN OUTLINE

WITH NUMEROUS ILLUSTRATIONS

BY

REV. C. H. TYNDALL

Pastor Broome Street Tabernacle, New York City

INTRODUCTION BY REV. A. F. SCHAUFFLER, D.D.

FLEMING H. REVELL COMPANY.
NEW YORK: | CHICAGO:
30 Union Square: East. | 148-150 Madison Street.
Publishers of Evangelical Literature.

Copyright, 1891

FLEMING H. REVELL COMPANY

The Carton Press
171, 173 Macdougal Street, New York

INTRODUCTION.

Much has been said and written about the use of the eye in impressing spiritual truth on an audience. But in spite of all the talk on this matter, outside of the Sunday-school little has been done, chiefly because many have not known how to get to work to enlist the eyes of their hearers. Pastors have acknowledged the power of object sermons, and have wished that they could prepare them, but have not felt that they dared launch out in this line of effort.

I am persuaded that we all have much to learn in the direction of using things material to impress things spiritual on the minds of our hearers. In any secular lecture, we see scientific men making just as constant use of the eye as possible, and we recognize that this is one of the sources of the delight that is experienced in listening to what they have to say, and one great means by which we remember that to which we have listened. While the lecturer is appealing to the eye, and at the same time is explaining what he shows, to the ear, he has the undivided attention of all in his audience. It is simply impossible to be carried away by wandering thoughts, while eye and ear are both being appealed to by the speaker. Since these are facts that no one contraverts, why should we not avail ourselves of the same methods in our pulpit utterances, and, by the use of both of our most rapid senses, do all we can to impress the truth on our hearers? If our Master preached from the text of a little child held in His arms, or taught the duty of humility by actually waiting on the table, why should we be so finical that we cannot lay aside our dignity, and use any method that will impress the truth on others? I am by no means advocating such a use of objects as shall merely attract attention to themselves and thus overlay the truth, for to do that is folly. But there is a most legitimate way of using material objects, and to that I desire to call renewed attention. Having myself used this kind of preaching and having found it helpful in a spiritual way, I can all the more heartily commend it to others.

The book for which I have written these few words by way of an introduction, is by my good friend Rev. C. H. Tyndall, the pastor of the Broome Street Tabernacle, of New York. Some of the sermons I have had the privilege of hearing, and I can bear witness to their spiritual effect on the audience. Of others I have the witness of those who have heard them, that they chained the attention of the audience and resulted in much good. They are worked out under the rules of Christian common-sense, which must govern here, as in all Christian work. It is the lack of just this "sixth sense" that has discredited so much of the blackboard and object work in this land. The reader will here find no folly that is calculated to repel him.

Of course, in the delivery of these sermons some practice will be found needful; but that is the case with everything good that is also new. But very soon any man with ordinary common-sense will find that the work becomes not only easy, but pleasant as well, and his audience will be delighted with the result. This will be especially true of the young people, who will flock to such services when the ordinary sermon fails to attract them. Some trouble is requisite in the preparation for a few of these sermons; but if any man wants a good thing without trouble, he is forever doomed to disappointment. The better a thing is, as a rule, the harder it is to attain. It is very easy to be stupid, but to be bright costs effort.

I would suggest that a right use of the sermons given in this book would be, not to preach them all on consecutive Sunday evenings, but to have an evening a month known as "Object-Sermon Sunday," and to advertise it as such, so that your people may know what they are to expect. If things go with the reader as they have with the writer, he will find that on that evening he will always have the largest audience of the month.

Finally, after having gained some facility in the use of the material thus prepared by another, let the preacher begin to prepare his own object sermons, beginning with simple ones, and going on to those that are more complex. At the same time let him remember, it is the simple things that are the most powerful. Simplicity, therefore, should be studied at all times, for in it there is power.   A. F. SCHAUFFLER.

CONTENTS.

	PAGE
INTRODUCTION,	5
OBJECT SERMONS IN THE BIBLE,	11

PART FIRST.

Sermons Referring Principally to the Unconverted.

I. THE PUMPS, Isa. 12 : 3,	25
II. THE LADDERS, John 10 : 1 ; Gen. 28 : 12,	31
III. THE PRINCIPLE OF DEATH IN THE SOUL OF THE SINNER, Eph. 2 : 1,	38
IV. CHLORINE GAS, Isa. 1 : 16–20,	46
V. STONES THAT TALK, Joshua 24 : 27 ; Hab. 2 : 11 ; Luke 19 : 40,	55
VI. CARBON, John 3 : 6,	65
VII. THE LIFE THAT WILL STAND, Ps. 1 : 5 ; Phil. 4 : 1,	69
VIII. LESSONS FROM A FROG,	78
IX. THE OLD DRY BONES, Ezek. 37 : 1–10,	84
X. THE STRIKING CONTRAST BETWEEN THE BREAD OF THE DEVIL AND THE BREAD OF THE LORD ILLUSTRATED, Isa. 55 : 2,	92
XI. THE ELECTRIC INDICATOR, Rom. 5 : 18,	102
XII. OUR BROKEN PLANK, Prov. 15 : 24,	106
XIII. EMBLEMS OF TIME AND JUSTICE, Ecc. 8 : 5,	110
XIV. BREAD, John 6 : 35,	115

PART SECOND.

Sermons Referring Principally to Christians.

XV.	THE LAMPS, Matt. 25 : 1–13,	118
XVI.	TESTING BY FIRE, Mal. 3 : 2, 3,	125
XVII.	CORN, John 15 : 8,	131
XVIII.	CRADLES, I. Cor. 13 : 11,	136
XIX.	THE SPIDER AND FLY, II. Tim. 2 : 26,	140
XX.	WONDERS OF THE SUN, Ps. 84 : 11,	145

PART THIRD.

Sermons Referring Principally to Children and Young People.

XXI.	LIGHT AND DARKNESS IN THE HEART, Eph. 5 : 8,	155
XXII.	THE VISIBLE AND INVISIBLE WRITING, Ecc. 12 : 14; I. Cor. 3 : 13,	160
XXIII.	THE WATCH, Ps. 139 : 14,	165
XXIV.	PAYING FOR GOD'S BENEFITS, Ps. 116 : 12, 13,	171
XXV.	THE STAR-FISH, Job 12 : 18,	177
XXVI.	THE BIRD'S NEST, Ps. 84 : 3,	182
XXVII.	HONEY, Ex. 3 : 8; Ps. 19 : 10,	186
XXVIII.	THE PRISM, Matt. 5 : 16,	188
XXIX.	IRON SHARPENING IRON, Prov. 27 : 17,	191
XXX.	A "YELLOW JACKET'S" OR WASP'S NEST, Prov. 6 : 6–8,	194
XXXI.	SAND, Deut. 33 : 19,	196
XXXII.	NEW WINE AND OLD BOTTLES, Luke 5 : 37–39,	199

XXXIII. THE KEY OF DAVID, Rev. 3 : 7, . . . 203
XXXIV. TESTING BY THE THERMOMETER,
   Lam. 3 : 40, ... 207
XXXV. THE FIERY DARTS, Eph. 6 : 16, . . 209
XXXVI. STONY HEARTS, Heb. 3 : 15, . . 212
XXXVII. THE ANCHOR, Heb. 6 : 19, . . . 214
XXXVIII. GROWTH OF THE POWER OF SIN,
   Isa. 28 : 22, ... 216
XXXIX. THE PEDOMETER, Eph. 4 : 1 ; Ps. 139 : 3, 220
XL. LIFE AND LIFE-LIKE, I. John 5 : 12, . 224
XLI. MASKS, Luke 8 : 17, ... 227
XLII. THE VEIL, II. Cor. 3 : 14, . . . 231
XLIII. THE CAUGHT MICE, Prov. 22 : 3, . 233
XLIV. THE FOOTSTOOL OF HIS FEET, Ps.
   110 : 1, ... 235
XLV. THE NAILS THAT FAIL, AND THE
   NAIL THAT HOLDS, Isa. 22 : 23, 24, . 238

PART FOURTH.

XLVI.—*Simple Objects Which May be Used as Illustrations in the Sunday-school and in Children's Meetings.*

GRASS, COMPASSES, ... 243
HUSKS, POTTAGE OR LENTILS, A FLAIL, THE
   MAGNET, ... 244
A CANDLE, SALT, CHAFF, SCARLET AND CRIMSON
   WOOL, ... 245
A SLING, A SWORD, A MAGNIFYING LENS, . . 246
A PHOTOGRAPH PLATE, A RIVET, A LEAF, . . 247
PRINCE RUPERT'S DROPS, A TOY BOOMERANG, . 248

THREE CUPS OF WATER, A CRUTCH,	249
A COMPASS, MUSTARD SEED, A COIN,	250
STUBBLE, FISHING TACKLE, PLATED SPOONS,	251
A PEAR, CASKS OR BOXES, PLATE GLASS, A BELT.	252
THE HAMMER, THE SQUARE, BALANCES, THE PLUMB LINE,	253
A JACK-PLANE AND SMOOTHING-PLANE, A COTTON STRING AND COPPER WIRE,	254

OBJECT SERMONS.

Object Sermons in the Bible.

A CHRISTIAN young man, who is a member of the church of which the author is pastor, came to the study one evening, and, during the conversation which ensued, stated that he liked object sermons very much, and was always pleased when they were announced. But he said he wondered if it were a scriptural method of preaching. He had been discussing the subject with a friend who held that there was nothing in the Bible authorizing it. It is not at all surprising that one should be unaware of the teaching of the Scripture on this subject, for it is a method so little used in ordinary sermons, that the examples given in the Scriptures attract very little attention from the casual reader. But when one has his attention called to the subject, he will be surprised to find to what an extent this style has been employed by God's servants, and many times under special divine command.

The object sermons contained in this book are generally of a simple nature. The plan was to have them just elaborate enough to gain the attention and impress the truth. A very simple object held in the hand will often accomplish this quite as well as a most elaborate one. This was the case with the sermon on the "Stones that Talk," when a wax cylinder from Edison's phonograph was held in the hand. All eyes were on that cylinder, and all ears were intently listening to what was said; and if we may judge from the inquirers in the after-meeting, the truth made its impression. But this attention and interest were, no doubt, largely due to the limited knowledge on the part of the audience concerning the phonograph. They had heard much about it, and wanted to know more. If an ordinary pocket knife had been held up, it would hardly have gained the attention for more then a few minutes, for every one is familiar with a knife. But if I did something with that knife which aroused the curiosity of the hearers, then all would be eager lookers and listeners.

By nature we all are curious. We cannot

see a crowd in the street unless it awakens a desire to know what is going on. Now, God has taken advantage of this tendency in man, to gain his attention to spiritual things; and in proportion as man's ears have become dull of hearing, and his eyes blinded to anything from God, in that proportion has He made use of striking object sermons. When, in the days of the prophet Ezekiel, Judah had sunken to nearly her lowest state religiously, many of the people having been carried away captive, and those who remained in Jerusalem being worse than those who were carried away, God commanded His prophet to employ the most striking symbols to gain the attention of His people. The truth never took so little hold upon them as now. The ordinary mode of presenting divine communication, was not sufficient to gain access for the Word. Therefore, more striking methods were employed. See how God commands Ezekiel, in the twelfth chapter of his prophecy, to prepare his stuff for removing, and remove by day in their sight, for He says, "It may be they will consider, though they be a rebellious house." "In their sight shalt thou bear it upon thy shoulders, and carry it forth in the twilight; thou shalt cover thy face, that thou see not the ground; for I have set thee for a sign unto the house of Israel. And I did so as I was commanded: I brought forth my stuff by day, as stuff for captivity, and in the even I digged through the wall with mine hand, and in the morning the word of the Lord came unto me, saying, Son of man, hath not the house of Israel, the rebellious house, said unto thee, *What doest thou?* Say, I am your sign: like as I have done, so shall it be done unto them; they shall remove and go into captivity."

And in the same chapter, at the seventeenth verse, he is commanded to eat bread with quaking, and drink water with trembling and with carefulness, and to say to the people that so should Israel eat bread with carefulness, and drink water with astonishment, because of their violence.

In the fourth chapter, Ezekiel tells how he was directed to take a tile, and draw the city of Jerusalem upon it, and lay a siege against the city, and set the camp against it, and set battering rams against it round about. This also was to be a sign to the house of Israel. Again, he was to lie upon his left side many days, and then turn and lie upon his right side for a certain length of time. "I have appointed thee each day for a year," in which Israel and Judah must bear their captivity, the one three hundred and ninety years, and the other forty years.

In the twenty-first chapter he tells us how the Lord told him to go out and set his face toward Jerusalem, and to drop his sword toward the city and its holy places, and say, "A sword, a sword is sharpened and also furbished." This is to indicate how God had appointed the ruin of the city. This symbol is carried throughout the chapter. In the twenty-fourth chapter he is to put a caldron over the fire, and to take of the bones of the choicest of the flock and put them into the pot, and pour on water, and let them seethe, till a scum comes upon the water. "Woe to the bloody city, to the pot whose scum is therein, and whose scum is not gone out of it!" "Therefore thus saith the Lord God, Woe to the bloody city! I will even make the pile for fire great. Heap on wood, kindle the fire, consume the flesh, and spice it well, and let the bones be burned. Then set it empty upon the coals thereof, that the brass of it may be hot, and may burn, and that the filthiness of it may be molten in it, that the scum of it may be consumed. She hath wearied herself with lies, and her great scum went not forth out of her; her scum shall be in the fire."

In the same chapter the death of Ezekiel's wife is to be used as a striking lesson to Israel. "Son of man, behold, I take away from thee the desire of thine eyes, with a stroke; yet neither shalt thou mourn nor weep, neither shall thy tears run down. . . . At even my wife died; and I did in the morning as I was commanded. And the people said unto me, Wilt thou not tell us what these things are to us, that thou doest so?" Then he informs them that as he has done in his mourning, so shall Israel do when their destruction comes upon them. It will be so great that it will preclude mourning, such as is usual when calamity is partial. There can be no doubt that this death was an historical fact, and was used, as indicated, to impress a most important truth upon the minds of those whom God loved, and whom He wished to bring to realize why they were thus caused to suffer, when they should be in exile and mourning.

Jeremiah frequently uses this method of teaching the people. In the thirteenth chapter, he tells how he was directed of the Lord to take a linen girdle or apron, and hide it in a cleft of a rock, and, after leaving it there for a long time, to go and take it again, in its ruined state, and show it to the people. Linen was the material of the priestly dress, and Israel was to be spiritually a kingdom of priests. "It was at once to symbolize the character of the people of Israel, stiff and impure, like unwashed linen, and to suggest the fate in store for it."

Under the type of a potter, he shows, in the eighteenth chapter, God's absolute power in disposing of the nations. And many since his time have learned lessons from the clay on the potter's wheel. In the nineteenth chapter, he preaches a very striking object sermon, when he gets a potter's vessel, and goes to the east gate of the city, and there proclaims to the people their sins, then breaks the potter's vessel, so that it cannot be made whole again, and declares that in such a manner God will rend Israel, so that they cannot be healed.

In the twenty-fourth chapter, God teaches Jeremiah a lesson, using as symbols two baskets of figs, one good and the other bad. "Then said the LORD unto me, What seest thou, Jeremiah? and I said, Figs; the good figs, very good; and the evil, very evil, that cannot be eaten, they are so evil. Thus saith the LORD, the God of Israel: Like these good figs, so will I acknowledge them that are carried away captive of Judah, whom I have sent out of this place into the land of the Chaldeans for their good. And as the evil figs, that cannot be eaten, they are so evil; surely thus saith the LORD, So will I give Zedekiah, the king of Judah, and his princes, . . . and I will deliver them to be removed into all the kingdoms of the earth for their hurt, to be a reproach and a proverb, a taunt and a curse, in all places whither I will drive them."

Under the type of bonds and yokes, Jeremiah, in the twenty-eighth chapter, prophesies of the subduing of the neighboring kingdoms to Nebuchadnezzar, and exhorts them to yield, and not to believe the false prophets.

We are given an impressive object lesson in the thirty-fifth chapter of Jeremiah. He calls in the Rechabites, and sets pots of wine before them, and tells them to drink. They refuse, saying that Jonadab, the son of Rechab, commanded them not to drink wine, and they have always obeyed his voice. Then the word of the LORD comes to Jeremiah saying, "Thus saith the LORD of hosts, the God of Israel. Go and tell the men of Judah and the inhabitants of Jerusalem, Will ye not receive instruction to hearken to my words? saith the LORD. The words of Jonadab the son of Rechab, that he commanded his sons not to drink wine, are performed; for unto this day they drink none, but obey their father's commandment: notwithstanding I have spoken unto you, rising early and speaking; but ye hearkened not unto me." In this striking way the prophet shows the people their great inconsistency in being deaf to the command of the Almighty God, their Father, while the Rechabites are very careful to obey their earthly father.

How striking must have been the act of Seraiah, the servant of Jeremiah, when he opened the book which contained the judgments of God against Babylon, and read those words, and then threw the book, with a stone tied to it, into the river Euphrates, and said, "Thus shall Babylon sink, and shall not rise"! Jer. 51:64.

How Jeroboam must have been impressed, when Ahijah, the prophet, clad in a new garment, met him in the field, and when they were alone, he caught the new garment, tore it in twelve pieces, and gave Jeroboam ten of them, explaining that thus the Lord would rend the kingdom of Solomon, and give ten tribes for him to rule over!

Many other passages similar to these might be referred to. Lest any one should consider this method belittling to the one who employs it, or lowering the office of the pulpit, it would be well to remember God's principal method of teaching spiritual truths in the Old Testament days, namely, by the sacrifices, and the tabernacle and the temple service generally. What were all these, but God's way of teaching spiritual truths by means of sensible objects? The slaying of every sacrificial lamb was to teach, and keep before the people, the spiritual truth of Jesus the Lamb of God, Who was to be slain for sinners. The sprinkled blood, the incense, the scapegoat, the altar, the ark of the covenant, the mercy seat, every article of clothing for the priests, and everything in and about the tabernacle, were for one and the same purpose—to teach the people, by these material objects, spiritual truths. And if God condescends thus in such minute details to use the most common things for the great and glorious purpose of teaching us divine lessons, no one need feel that he is belittling himself in adopting the same method.

The kindergarten system of instruction is nothing new. It was used long before Froebel lived. It reaches back to the Garden of Eden, when God began the instruction of our first parents by clothing them in the skins of animals which had no doubt been slain to teach them the first lesson in the sacrifice, which is the alpha of man's salvation.

There can be no doubt that Jesus, the greatest of all teachers, used this very method in His teachings. He called upon nature, all about His listeners, to teach them the most profound spiritual truths. It was not considered beneath His dignity to draw lessons from the most common household affairs: sweeping, using yeast in baking bread, the mustard seed, and the like. "Without a parable spake he not unto them."

That method of instruction for body and mind which, without doubt, is considered the best by the most skilled teachers in our schools and colleges, is according to the kindergarten system; and what is good instruction in a college is also good in a church, if we remember the two different objects that are being especially aimed at, the one principally intellectual, and the other principally spiritual. If society were perfect, our school would be sufficient, for all instruction would be for the physical, intellectual, and spiritual development of the pupil. But society is not perfect, and religious teachers must use the methods which are so successful in the best schools, if they would do the best work.

The preaching of these sermons has not been merely to attract the people, although many more have attended whenever such a sermon has been announced; but the object aimed at has been the religious instruction and the immediate conversion of the hearers. That they have made a deep impression on those who have heard them is evident to every careful observer of the results. Said a little girl to her Sunday-school teacher several months after she had listened to the Anchor sermon: "When I kneel down to pray at night, I wonder if my anchor is in the mud, and not in something solid." One Christian young lady who heard the Pump sermon, said to a friend afterward: "I think I am that pump which has to be primed and worked at so hard to get anything from it."

The impression made in the Ladder sermon by the ladder quietly descending down through the ceiling was very striking.

But the most marked result of these object sermons has been seen in the inquiry meeting, which is always held after the Sunday evening service. After preaching object sermons of from eight to ten minutes in length to the children every Sunday morning for about a year, some of our best workers requested me to extend the children's sermon to twenty-five minutes, and let it be the sermon for old and young. They frankly told me that they enjoyed them, and learned more from them than from the other sermons. I resolved, therefore, to preach such a sermon once a month. These have been continued for more than a year. I do not call to mind one evening meeting in which an object sermon has been preached, that there have not been inquirers in the second meeting; and often these after-meetings have been marked with special spiritual power. This is stated merely to show that the use of object sermons is for something besides attracting those who are curious to see what is going to be done.

One thing should be borne in mind—objects

should not be dwelt upon so long, or be so conspicuous, that the mind cannot be made to turn readily to the spiritual application. As a rule, I have so arranged at least half of the sermon, that the attention would not be called to the objects, but to that which they were designed to teach.

In giving them into the hands of the publisher, I do so, praying they may be taken and used by others with far greater power in the salvation of souls than they have been in my own ministry.

Literary merit is not claimed for these outlines. For whatever merit they may possess, or for any measure of helpfulness there may be found in them for others, the author would give thanks to Him whose name he would honor and whose grace and truth he would make known.

I.

The Pumps.

Therefore with joy shall ye draw water out of the wells of salvation. Isa. 12 : 3.

[Objects.—Six pumps on a long bench, two of them merely fastened to the bench; the third running down into a beer keg with red liquid in it; the fourth into a white pail with the words "Christ, World," painted on it, and with black water in it; the fifth running down into a pail having "Salvation" painted on it and pure water within it; the sixth, the same as the fifth. Paint on one edge of the bench the motto, "Draw from the well Salvation." Consider the pumps in order, and pump them as you speak of them.]

I. These two pump nothing; they are connected with no well, and so there is no water. They are non-professors of religion.

1. The large one is the finest of all the pumps—it is a perfect pump. It is one that makes a good show. Good lives are good things, but they are useless unless they are joined to Christ. Many people seem to lack but the one thing, and that is Christ. But with all their beauty, they are as useless as this pump when not connected with the water. Although it is a force pump, no one would think of going to it in case of fire.

2. The other has serious defects; besides not being connected with any water supply, there is little or no valve in it. So with many persons. It cannot be said that the one thing they lack is to receive Christ. There may be a certain amount of repairing necessary before they can draw up the water of life, such as putting away revengeful feelings, forgiving enemies, and making restoration and reparation as far as possible; yet all these things may be done, and the pump not be running down into the water. This is the main thing, and if this is done the others are quite likely to follow.

II. This one is connected below, but it is no great honor to it. It can say that it is at least connected with something, if nothing more than a beer keg. This is a person who has some kind of a form of religion; he goes to church once a year, and to funerals occasionally, when he cannot get rid of it. He may have some kind of a connection with some formal church, and that is about enough religion for him. And what he pumps up is well represented by the beer keg (it contains red liquid).

He is the one who makes his stomach his god. His appetite is his chief concern. He is a glutton or wine-bibber; the one who feeds his lust, who is sensual; or the one who lives for money.

All that such persons pump is the life-blood of their own and others' souls.

III. This is one who makes a more reasonable profession, and is not so bold-faced in sin.

He goes to meetings regularly, is always at the communion service, and attends the weekly prayer meeting occasionally, if it does not come upon a social or an evening he calls his out-night; he is the decent professor, who is in hand and glove with the world; the worldling in the church, whose motto could well be, "Christ and the world." The water that he draws is always black.

IV. This one is all right, is connected with the well Salvation; it has pure water in its well, and gives nothing but pure water. There is nothing at all against this one in any way. He is a Christian, and will, we hope, reach Heaven. But it is like pulling teeth to get any water out of him. He always has good excuses. If you get anything from him, you have to pump and pump and prime, and then get only a few drops, and they soon stop; but what he does pour out is good.

There is something wrong with the valves within all such pumps. The trouble is always within, and not without. There needs to be some repairing done by the Holy Spirit on all such Christians.

V. The "ready-at-once" pump, and always giving a good stream. This is a true Christian, and one always to be counted upon in an emergency, and who needs no priming and coaxing, praying and begging, and always does his duty, pouring out that which Christ puts within, for the benefit of others.

Lessons: 1. Before any water can be pumped up out of the earth, it must descend in the showers. But God has sent the showers already upon the thirsty land: Christ has come, the well Salvation.

2. All who are fully connected with this fountain, draw water from it with joy. This

drawing water from the fountain opened in the house of David for sin and uncleanness, is simply drinking in Jesus. Not merely drinking in of His spirit, temper, or mind, but drinking Him into the soul.

a. This drinking brings life eternal.

b. It brings a blessed communion with Him, which is a blessed foretaste of Heaven. This is the joy of the text.

c. It brings likeness to Him, both in character and in the imparting of this water to others, for all who come to Him and drink have rivers of living water flowing from them to others.

3. But to give forth any water, there must be a connection made with Him, the fountain.

There are many spurious springs, which seem at first to promise much. The name of such is legion, and they are, according to prophecy, increasing more and more. There are so many "dry in the summer" wells. But there is only one Living Fountain; so be careful to what spring you go.

4. To get the true water, one must get down. Living water is not taken from the surface. Men need to get low down to get this water. God knows the proud afar off; water is found by getting down to it. The great things of earth are obtained by climbing: this by the opposite.

5. In vain is it to rattle the pump in time of dearth or fire, if it has not been previously connected with the fountain. Many will cry in the awful day for water, but will find none in themselves, for connection with Christ was neglected. You will go to an awful desert if you provide no water beforehand. Have this water within, and yours will be a land ever green and glorious, and you shall walk by the river of the water of life, and draw from the wells of salvation, with eternal joy.

II.

The Ladders.

He that entereth not by the door into the sheepfold, but climbeth up some other way, the same is a thief and a robber. John 10: 1.

And he dreamed, and behold a ladder set up on the earth, and the top of it reached to Heaven: and behold the angels of God ascending and descending on it. Gen. 28: 12.

[OBJECTS.—When this sermon was delivered, the ladders were from five to ten feet in length, excepting the one that represented Jacob's ladder, which was forty or more feet in length. This ladder was made of two ropes, one being white cotton and the other being common hemp, representing the humanity and divinity in Christ. The rounds were about a foot in length, painted red. They were tied to the ropes. This ladder was so arranged that it was silently dropped from the ceiling when Jacob's ladder was mentioned, the lower end resting on the platform by the speaker, and the upper end disappearing from view in a little opening in the ceiling. All the others were brought to the speaker as needed. The effect of the sudden and striking contrast between these and Jacob's ladder was remarkable.]

There are many ways that people have which they think will get them into Heaven. Bunyan's Christian saw two men, Formalist and Hypocrisy, come tumbling over the wall on the left hand of the narrow way. Some now try to climb up some other way. Notice some of the different ladders upon which men try to climb to Heaven.

I. The white ladder represents a good, pure, moral, honest life. The one with this ladder is not guilty of defrauding any one. Such a life is to be desired, but is a poor thing to climb to Heaven on. It is too short, and has nothing to lean against, and also, it has a round broken out. The most pure white ladder on earth has this same defect; "for all have sinned and come short of the glory of God." This ladder is ruled out; "for by the works of the law shall no flesh be justified."

II. Here is the black ladder. It is not a very attractive one. It represents the one who hopes to climb up to Heaven on the faults of others; the one who is congratulating himself that he is better than many church members. He knows many hypocrites, and he will stand a better show than they. God says to this one: "Therefore thou art inexcusable. O man whosoever thou art that judgest: for wherein thou judgest another thou condemnest thyself; for thou that judgest doest the same things." The white ladder failed; how much more this!

III. Here is the red ladder. This is the one who believes most thoroughly in the need and power of the blood of Christ. He has had a good early training, and values it very highly. He knows the whole plan of salvation, and is very familiar with the Bible; you can tell him little or nothing new in the Scripture. He knows that all men are sinners, and cannot be saved by their own goodness. He knows that all must repent, and believe in Christ, if they are to be saved. He is a most thoroughly orthodox man, and would be offended to be told otherwise. He says that he does believe in Christ, and does not trust to his own goodness to save him at all. What more can be asked of him? Saving faith is not believing about Christ: the devils also believe, and tremble. Saving faith is trust in Christ as a person, and not believing something about Him. The wrath of God is revealed against all who hold the truth in unrighteousness; so this ladder is also too short.

IV. The gold ladder is a fine one. It represents the wealth and refinement of the world. The one who possesses this is a lady or gentleman. He is kind and polite to all. He is high in office, or in the estimation of all who know him. When a great statesman or rich man dies, we are liable to think he must have gone to Heaven. But greatness is not the ladder to reach Heaven on. "Except a man be born again, he cannot see the kingdom of God." This ladder too is a failure.

V. The black-and-white ladder, with the last three rounds broken, is the ladder of good resolution. On the first of the year, or a birthday, or on some other special occasion he turns over a new leaf. He makes strong resolutions and very encouraging prom ises. He seems to go well for a time, but soon a round is cracked, the next one breaks worse still, and that which began so white, ends black. He is ever expecting to be better in the future, but is procrastinating his becoming a Christian. But the very fact that he is some time going to be one, is a means of great comfort to him. So the foolish virgins intended to go into the marriage, but did not. No one ever reached Heaven on one of these ladders.

VI. This is a very different ladder from all the others, in that it can stand alone as none of them can do. As a step-ladder around the house, it is very convenient. The red below represents right belief.  The white above represents good, pure works. This is man's idea of the church. Many think that there is something about membership with the church that makes them secure for the future. There is no doubt that the church is a great means of help to a Christian; but to one who is not, and is using it as a ladder to get to Heaven on, it is a hindrance, and not a help. Christ, and not the church, is the door into Heaven. No one has membership with the true church who has not entered by the door. The useful step-ladder is too short to be saved on, and is also ruled out.

VII. This brings us to the ladder which Jacob saw a vision of in his dream, the one that reached down from Heaven to the earth. On it the angels ascended and descended.

Christ is the ladder (John 1 : 51), and God's mercies are the angels; for every mercy man has received has come down this ladder. All has been done for His sake, whether before He came or since. This too, is the only ladder that leads up out of the dark pit of sin to Heaven.

To be saved by it you must: 1. Take hold of it. It is not enough to be near to Christ, or to know about Him—you must lay hold of Him as your own. 2. You must let go of all other ladders. Cling to nothing but Him. 3. You must hold on. And you must hold on, too, with both hands. Holding on to the world, or any sin, with one hand, and Christ with the other, would be an utter failure, if such a thing were possible. 4. Don't cut yourself off with any sin, great or small, for a moment, for there is an awful gulf below you. 5. Keep on climbing. It is not enough to run well for a time. "Jacob's Ladder," on the island of St. Helena, has seven hundred steps. Thousands start to go up, and they usually start on a run, but only a few ever go all the way up. Remember: Take hold; hold on; keep on climbing. Now the ladder drops down before you. Christ is now before your heart. Will you receive Him? Lay hold while you may. Soon the darkness will come. The Saviour will soon be the Judge.

III.

The Principle of Death in the Soul of the Sinner.

Dead in trespasses and sins.   Eph. 2 : 1.

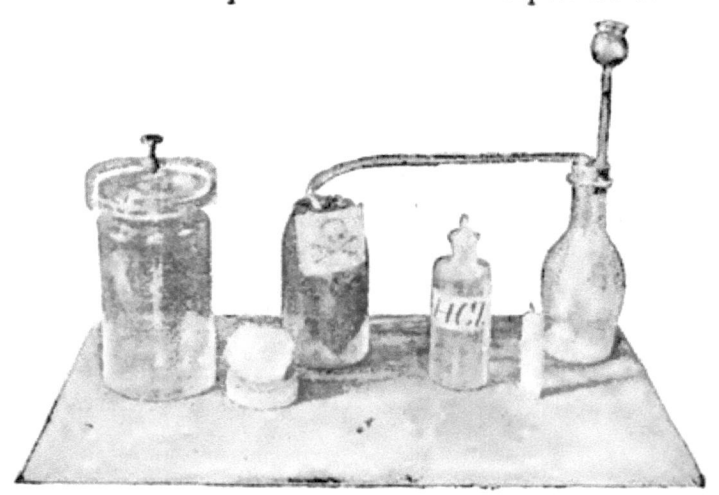

[OBJECTS.—Two fruit jars, a candle, a piece of marble, some hydrochloric acid, some glass tubing, and a large-mouthed bottle. Put some small fragments of marble into the bottle, and pour on water about one quarter of an inch in depth. Put a cork in the bottle, having two small glass tubes running through it. One is bent after leaving the cork so that it can be placed in one of the fruit jars. The other glass tube should have a little funnel on one end, so that the acid can be poured into it. The other end of this tube should extend down into the water within one-eighth of an inch of the bottom of the bottle. Pour some of the acid into the bottle, and at once the carbonic acid gas is liberated, and as soon as the bottle is full it will fill the fruit jar. If a candle, or a lighted stick be lowered into this, it will be quenched at once. The light should be allowed to burn in the jar before the CO_2 is put into the jar, so that it will not be thought that there was something in it before.]

I. I hold in my hand a piece of common marble. There is in it a principle of death. So I am told by text-books on chemistry. One cannot tell that there is such a thing about it by looking at it, by handling it, or tasting it. You might break it into small pieces, finer than flour, and still you could not see anything about it that you could call a principle of death. But chemistry says that there is such a mysterious thing about it, and you would be foolish to deny it on any such an examination as one can give who is not instructed by the text-books.

So the Bible tells us that our souls, by nature, are dead. We cannot see the death, we cannot feel it. You cannot tell by looking at a person whether he is a Christian or not. Those who have this death in the soul, which the Bible says all men have by nature, may look and act just like any one who has spiritual life within him. Until we have a better way of telling—and we shall never have in this life—we must believe what the Text-Book on this subject tells us. That tells us that our soul is dead in trespasses and in sins.

II. We will unlock the death in this marble, and so confirm what is declared to be in it. We put this lighted candle into the fruit jar and notice that it burns all right: it can live in the jar. This is because of the presence of enough oxygen there to feed the flame. (If quite a quantity of hydrochloric acid be poured into the bottle, on the marble, the CO_2 will be given off rapidly, and will fill the jar.) Now we have enough of the death principle to test, and yet you cannot see anything. But lower the lighted candle, and see the strange effect on that. It extinguishes it at once. Just as often as we try it, just so often it puts it out. It will kill the flame of a lighted stick that has been saturated in oil. Now, the death principle in the marble, as a part of it, has manifested itself in the strange way of extinguishing lights, and we have confirmed the teaching of the text-book on the subject.

So the death in the unconverted person's soul is the reason for certain strange and otherwise unaccountable things.

1. This is the reason it is so dangerous for a Christian person to be very intimately associated with one who is not. The light of the Christian is quenched by the death in his friend. There are multitudes of cases which any observing person might cite, in which the light of a Christian has gone out because of an unchristian associate. Shun the deadly atmosphere. Your soul cannot live in it.

2. This is why some persons will choose a short period of time in which to be happy instead of an unlimited time. Like the "rich fool" mentioned in the gospels, they prefer pleasures for a brief moment to those that are unending. Here they know that they can stay but a short time, and yet they irrationally choose the brief, in preference to the everlasting pleasures at God's right hand.

3. This is why some so strangely prefer their enemy to their friend—Satan to Christ. They can see nothing of beauty in Him. I have a check in my hand. It was sent me by a friend. You might look at it, and you would see that it is for eighty-five dollars payable to my order; and that is all you would see, except the signature. But I can see in it: a friend of mine carried by the railroad on a journey, and

housed, fed with dainties, made very happy, and returned home again. I see all this more than you can, because I am looking at it with a different eyesight than you are. Some persons have no eyesight to see the attractiveness of Christ.

4. This death in the soul is the reason why men are more afraid of one another than they are of God. The man in Christ's parable was "afraid," and went and hid his talent in the earth. He was not as much afraid of his Master as he ought to have been, or he would not have done so. Unconverted persons are often afraid to become Christians, but it is a fear of what man may think, rather than what God thinks. It is strange that one should be more afraid of poor, weak man than of the Almighty. It can be accounted for only by considering it a result of the death in the soul.

5. This, too, is why one will so often hazard everything for nothing. When the *Pioneer Press*, of Minneapolis, burned in 1890, the bells were ringing, but many of the editors and others continued their work, and soon found to their horror that their way of escape was cut off. The loss of life was due to a careless spirit on the part of some of them. But they hoped to gain something in getting their work done. Many unchristian persons do not expect to gain anything by refusing longer to

yield to Christ, and still they continue to risk their all, with no hope of gain for doing it. The death principle within them makes them act in this strange and inconsistent way.

III. So there must be a change. This is not an arbitrary thing that Christ demands, but is a necessity. When I say to this jar, "There must be a change in the nature of your contents, or you will always have within you the principle of death," you can readily see that in saying this I am not making an arbitrary demand. So, when Jesus says that except a man be born again, or from above, by the Holy Spirit, He is not making an arbitrary demand, but is speaking of an absolute necessity of the soul.

Now I step up to this jar of carbonic acid gas, and breathe into it, and there comes into it another principle; and as I lower the lighted candle, it burns without any difficulty. There has been a change in the contents of the jar, by the coming in of a new principle, which drove out the old principle of death.

When God created man, he breathed into his nostrils, and he became a living soul. By his sin man caused the Divine Spirit of life to depart from him. He could return to man only as the sin he (man) had committed, was atoned for by the death of Christ. The atonement of Christ being an accomplished fact, now

He can return to the soul, and man must be born again by Him, or he cannot see life. The Greek word for spirit is *pneuma*, breath, from *pneuo*, to breathe. As God breathed once, so He must breathe again, into the dead soul of man, and the coming in of that Divine Spirit, or Breath, drives out the spirit of death. So, becoming a Christian, is not a matter of instruction, or good conduct, or anything that the sinner can do himself. It is the coming in of a new life, as I breathed a new principle into the jar, only the Breath that comes into the soul is a divine living person, and not merely a principle. Many do not know this, and they struggle all their lives to do for themselves what can only be done for them by God. This birth must be from above.

IV. For the jar to remain as it was before, is to remain with death within. To remain as you are is to remain dead to God. The father said of his prodigal son, "This my son was dead," yet he was alive in one sense. "He that believeth [receiveth] not the Son, shall not see life; but the wrath of God abideth [or remaineth] on him." You have not to wait twenty years to be dead to God: you are dead already.

V. The unlocking day is coming. As the acid unlocked the carbonic acid gas from the marble, so God will put in His key, and the spiritual death will be strikingly manifest. In that day we shall not have to depend alone on what the Bible, the text-book on this subject, tells us, nor upon what manifestations we can see in this world, of that death within the soul, but it will then be manifest before the whole universe of souls. So, be ready for that day by receiving the Spirit of divine life now.

IV.

CHLORINE GAS.

Put away the evil of your doings from before mine eyes ; cease to do evil ; learn to do well ; . . . come now, and let us reason together, saith the Lord ; though your sins be as scarlet, they shall be as white as snow; though they be red like crimson, they shall be as wool. . . . But if ye refuse and rebel, ye shall be devoured. Isa. 1 : 16-20.

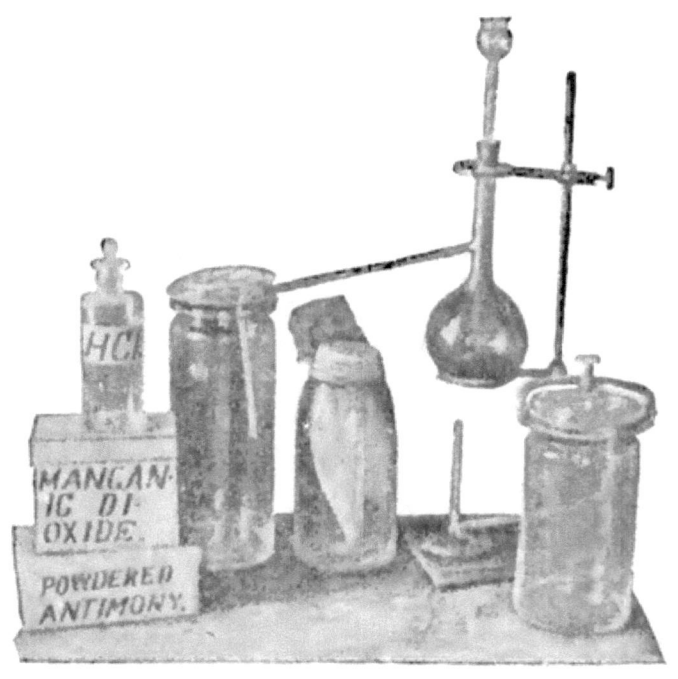

[OBJECTS.—A flask with a large neck; a tight-fitting cork, through which run two glass tubes, one down very near to the bottom, so as to be covered with the liquid, and the other bent so that it can be put into a jar. Rubber tubing may be used instead of all glass for this tube if desired. For the jars to receive the gas, two quart fruit jars will do. Put into the flask an ounce or two of manganic dioxide (or black oxide of manganese), and add three times its weight of hydrochloric acid. When this is gently heated, chlorine gas will fill the jars. This is heavier than the air, and so settles in the bottom. Call attention to the fact that you can see nothing in the jars.

Light a wax taper, not a candle unless it be a small one with a large wick (the taper is better), and lower it into one of the jars of chlorine. It extinguishes the flame, but at once relight it, and it burns with a red flame, and sends up a large volume of smoke. The flame is extinguished as soon as it is brought out to the air again. This may be repeated several times, or as long as the jar of chlorine lasts. Dampen some red tissue paper, or colored flowers, and suspend them in the second jar of chlorine, and they will be decolorized in a few moments. Into the third jar sprinkle some powdered antimony or arsenic, and it will fall to the bottom in a shower of sparks; a piece of phosphorus will also take fire in this gas. Any one or all of these can be used. The chlorine gas *should not* be exposed to the sunlight, as it will explode. The odor of this gas is very strong. The performing of this experiment is very simple, but one always needs to try it well beforehand to know just what he can do. Light a taper and put it into the jar.]

I. The first thing we noticed when the lighted taper was put into the jar of chlorine was that it was extinguished. Every person is shining with some kind of a light. We are told in Prov. 20: 27 that the spirit of man is the candle of the Lord. But that candle has had the divine light extinguished, and it has been lighted by Satan, by whose power it shines. The foolish virgins who did not get into the marriage supper had a light at the beginning, which finally went out. Prov. 24: 20 says, "The candle of the wicked shall be put out." Isa. 50: 11 (R. V.) says: "Behold, all ye that kindle a fire, that gird yourselves about with fire-brands: walk ye in the flame of your fire, and among the brands that ye have kindled. This shall ye have of mine hand; ye shall lie down in sorrow."

Who can doubt that unconverted persons have a light? But it is a false light, which leads to ruin; and how many it allures that way! What a light in any place is a saloon! How it gathers its victims about it, as moths are gathered about a candle, only to be ruined. Just so every unconverted person is a light to those about him. His light is his manner of life, his doings. By these he draws associates, and leads them on into the darkness of sin. Every father or mother is a light to the child. The boy wants to be like his father; and if that father is not a Christian, he is a false light to lead the boy to ruin. A boy saw his father drinking whiskey and said, "Papa, you drink whiskey, and when I get big I'll drink whiskey too." Judah, in the days when Isaiah wrote this text, had a light, but it was an exceedingly evil one, for their works were evil. We are to let our light so shine before men that they, seeing our *good* WORKS, will glorif your Father in Heaven. Good works are the shining of a good light, evil works are the shining of an evil light. So the text says, "put away the evil of your doings." And the first thing God does for any one who comes to him is to put out his light. What a blessed thing it would be if the light of every sinful person were put out, if all the will-o'-the-wisps were destroyed; but "the light of the wicked shall be put out, and the spark of his fire shall not shine" (Job 18:5).

The light is put out, that it may burn with the right kind of a flame. You noticed with what a different color the taper burned after it was extinguished and relighted. God wants no one to put away the evil of his doing that he may do nothing, but that he may do even more. How strikingly true this was with Saul of Tarsus, who became Paul the Apostle, when his light had been quenched, and then relighted! How he afterward shone for God's glory, even more brightly than he had for His dishonor before!

The wax taper burns with two different flames, because these flames are produced from two entirely different sources. At first it depends on the oxygen in the air to feed the flame; and when in the jar, hydrogen and chlorine feed the flame. So the Christian draws his power for light from a new source, when he is relighted.

The burning taper was extinguished as soon as it was brought out of the jar. It could burn only in that gas. No one can shine with the divine light except as he remains in Christ. "If a man abide not in me, he is cast forth as a branch, and is withered."

This shining is done also only *through* Christ. The taper shines in the jar of chlorine, and through it. There is no good deed done except through Christ. Men do so love to shine all by themselves, that it may be seen how good or great they are! But all of our little lights must be put out, and the Spirit of God will light us, and let us shine for Christ's honor. God kills us, our work, our light, that He may make us alive, that He may make us shine; and there is no life, and there can be no true light, in us till this is done.

II. There is another power in this chlorine besides that of extinguishing and relighting the taper. When we come to Christ we are, the best of us, like this red paper, "red like crimson." We are dead to God, and full of our own shining. We need not only relighting, but purifying. That is just what the chlorine does to this paper. (Dampen the paper and suspend it in the jar of chlorine.)

1. Nothing but the Holy Spirit can purify us. We cannot do it for ourselves, any more than this paper can for itself. We will fail as much here as we would to try to relight our soul with the divine life. Too often men are saved through faith, and then think they are to be kept saved by their own works. We are saved through faith, and also sanctified through faith in Christ by the Holy Spirit.

2. The red paper must remain in the chlorine, for this is a gradual process, and not an instantaneous thing like the lighting. Many Christians become discouraged because they are not made perfect at once. They are not willing to have the bleaching process go on step by step. Many stop and retard the work by their not abiding in the presence of God. There is not enough communion with Christ in the closet. Their study of, and meditation on, the Word of God is very brief; and it is no wonder they do not get on well, for they are so little in the company of Christ that His grace does not have a fair chance at their hearts. There is too much remaining very near the dividing line between spiritual life and spiritual death. So there may be a flame, but there is so little power there that the work of grace is retarded.

4. I suppose this paper has no feeling, and so does not feel at all irritated that its color is so rapidly disappearing. This is not the case with us. To get the stain of sin out of our souls, is often a crucifying work, and we need to hold still until it is done. The old nature does not die easily, and God often has to use sufferings, persecutions, afflictions, or poverty. The Psalmist says, "Before I was afflicted I went astray." It requires these things to come to us often, to make us remain with

God. So, hold still, if you would be made better.

5. Here it is, made white. So it will be with you if you abide in Christ. The perfect day will come soon. "Though your sins be as scarlet, they shall be as white as snow." Every vestige of sin will be gone, and you will be as pure as though you had never sinned in word, thought, or deed, for you shall be like Him.

III. Notice that this powdered antimony (or arsenic) put into the presence of this gas is immediately consumed. Every soul who does not seek Christ in this life, and experience His quenching and relighting power, and pass through His cleansing process, will still have to meet Him, but it will be meeting Him as Judge and not as Saviour and Sanctifier. "But if ye refuse and rebel, ye shall be devoured." "For our God is a consuming fire." Moses at the burning bush had to remove his shoes from off his feet because of the presence of God. The men of Beth-shemesh to the number of 50,070 were slain for looking into the ark, the symbol of God's presence. Christ says men shall cry for rocks and mountains to fall on them, to hide them from the face of Him that sitteth on the throne.

Now, Christ waits to impart His divine light and life, and to purify by His presence from every sin. Every soul must choose between this, and being consumed by Him when He "shall be revealed from Heaven, with His mighty angels, in flaming fire, taking vengeance on them that know not God and that obey not the gospel of our Lord Jesus Christ."

V.

STONES THAT TALK.

And Joshua said unto all the people, Behold, this stone shall be a witness unto us; for it hath heard all the words of the Lord which he spake unto us: it shall be therefore a witness unto you, lest ye deny your God. Joshua 24: 27.

For the stone shall cry out of the wall, and the beam out of the timber shall answer [margin *witness against*] *it.* Hab. 2: 11.

If these should hold their peace, the stones would immediately cry out. Luke 19: 40.

[OBJECTS.—A wax cylinder from Edison's phonograph, or a plate from Berliner's gramophone; an ordinary daguerrotype picture, or tintype, and some phosphorescent paper usually put in match-safes, or some punk from the wood.]

I. There is a sense in which these texts are literally true, and the lesson we wish to draw from them is that our actions, our words, and even our thoughts make an indelible impression on everything about us.

1. I hold in my hand a cylinder from Edison's phonograph. This is put into the phonograph, and, as it is turned, one speaks, and the sound vibrations cause a little membrane, having a small needle-like point on one side, to vibrate and puncture very tiny holes into the wax cylinder. These little holes represent the speech, for if the cylinder is put on the phonograph again, and a needle fastened to a membrane is made to fall into these same holes, the same sound will be reproduced. This wax then catches the sound, and holds on to it, perhaps for years, till the master of the phonograph compels it to give up its secret.

Not only the vibrations, which are registered in the wax by the needle, make an impression on the wax, but every vibration that falls upon it is registered there, and, if we had a phonograph sufficiently delicate and sensitive, we could reproduce it. And what is true of wax is also true of every object about us. So when

Joshua said, "This stone ... hath heard all the words," and Jesus said, "The stones would immediately cry out," they uttered what we all may yet hear take place. All the objects of the world about us are God's phonographs. And the sounds of our speech, which leave their impress upon the matter about us, the force of which men say can never be lost, may yet be reproduced to our wondering ears, when God shall make His phonographs give up their secrets. Whatever words you speak, you can say to yourself, "I shall probably hear this again."

2. But all our words do not fall upon the things just about us: they go on out into the atmosphere, just as the wave vibrations in the sea go on. Of course these vibrations become slower and slower as they move on in their journey, which never ends. Our ears can hear those as sound that are between 16 and 38,000 a second; all that are more or less we cannot hear. As the sounds of our words go out into space, the sound waves soon become so slow that we, or any other human being, cannot hear them. But they are there, and we must not think they cannot be heard at all. God hears them. Sound travels at the rate of 1,150 feet in a second, or about 18,000 miles in a day, and nearly 7,000,000 miles in a year. So it would take it 13 years to reach the sun,

70 years to reach Jupiter, 130 to reach Saturn, 250 to reach Uranus, and 400 years before it would reach Neptune. It would have to travel on for 17,000 years before it would reach Sirius, the brightest star seen. But God is everywhere, and hears it all the while it is on its journey. There is not an instant that He does not hear all that has ever passed the lips of man; for all these words are going on somewhere yet. You may ask, "Have not these waves of sound become so slow that they cannot even be heard by God?" Here Edison's wax cylinder can teach us another lesson. He says that the phonograph can receive ten vibrations, or less, in a second, which no human ear can hear, and then, by raising the pitch, you could hear those inaudible whispers in a loud, clear tone, as loud as you care to make them. If the phonograph can thus make the inaudible whispers heard in strong tones, what can not God do in the same way? He hears the words that have been spoken ever since man was on the earth. The groans of Christ's sufferings are as distinctly heard as ever, and they will never cease to ring in God's ears as they continue their endless journey. In the other world, where our ears will be sharper than they are here, God may permit us to hear all the words we have ever spoken. The universe is a phonograph which treasures up all

we say, and will soon speak it off to us, and the words to many will be startlingly familiar.

II. We make an impression on the universe not only by sound, but also by light.

1. Here is a photograph, commonly known as a tintype. It is in reality a picture upon iron that has been rolled very thin, and then been coated over with a material that is very sensitive to the light. The rays of light were going out from these buildings in thousands of directions, carrying pictures of the buildings with them; and a camera with this small piece of iron in it, was placed in the track of some of these rays, and they left this image imbedded into the silvered surface of the tintype. It is safe to say that a million pictures could have been taken at the time this was, of these buildings, if there had been that number of cameras pointed at them, and every picture would have been some different from the others. This shows the countless number of pictures that the rays of light carry away from every object on which they fall. If they fall upon any objects, such as glass, iron, stone, wood, or paper, that are properly guarded, as they are in the camera, and covered with a solution of silver, then they leave an image of the object there.

2. Light makes an impression on many objects that are not coated with a solution of sil-

ver. Here is a match-safe that has the following reading on the back: "Hang the safe where the letters may receive and absorb freely either the daylight or any artificial light, and they will shine in the darkness." Paint, paper, and many other objects are manufactured that have these same properties. Some fish, and decayed wood, have this phosphorescent power to a great extent. It is supposed that every object has this power of holding on to the rays of light which they receive, to a greater or less extent, or that they are more or less phosphorescent. "Nature is a wonderful conserver of what takes place in its realm. Science has been showing us of late something of the force residing in the actinic rays of light, by which it transfers impressions from one object to another. Wherever light goes it carries and leaves images. The trees mirror one another, and opposing mountains wear each the likeness of the other upon their rocky breasts."

If this is so, then the world is not only a phonographic cylinder for God to read, but is also a photographic plate for Him to look at. He is the great Developer, and the day may come when He will show us a perfect photograph of all our acts. We are recording our words, acts, and looks on everything about us. Just as some of the old parchments that have been found in monasteries with the writings of philosophers on the surface, and then after a while a process has been discovered that has brought out the prayers and praise of the early Christians written on the same skin, and then beneath that the blasphemous writings of pagans, and all is brought to light one after the other, so it may be with the most familiar objects about us. God may unroll, in the Judgment, one event after another of our lives that we thought were forgotten.

3. As we have already seen, the light carries in its rays a picture of everything on which it has fallen. So, the act that you perform now, the light catches up and carries out into space at the rate of 192,000 miles a second. On it goes, through the atmosphere and ether of space, to distant worlds. It will reach the sun in eight minutes, the planet Jupiter in fifty-two minutes, Uranus in two hours, Neptune in four hours and one-quarter, the star Vega in forty-five years, a star of the eighth magnitude not till one hundred and eighty years, and it will not reach a star of the twelfth magnitude till four thousand years. So light and sound are carrying the events of our lives one after another out into space, and they are being seen and heard by God all the time. David said, " My sin is ever before me." It certainly was literally ever before God, and was constantly crying to Him for punishment.

III. We have seen how we affect the universe by our words, acts, and looks. We just as truly make an impression on everything about us by our thoughts. We have instruments for measuring nearly everything. The thermometer measures the temperature, the barometer the invisible forces of the atmosphere, the galvanometer the minute electric current, and the spirometer measures the power of the lungs. So also there is an instrument proposed to measure the amount of physical energy required for a certain amount of thought. A writer in the *Scientific American* for March 21st, 1891, under the heading, "Electricity as a Measure of Thought," says: "It is well known to the medical profession that every mental effort causes a rush of blood to the brain, and that the amount of blood depends upon the intensity of the thought; but rush of blood means rise of temperature, and if we could measure this we would be able to determine, in a rough way, the power necessary for the generation of any thought or mental effort." This measuring is proposed to be done by means of a thermo-electric pile and a very sensitive galvanometer.

Whether it is possible to measure the physical energy required for a certain amount of thought or not, it is certainly true that one's thoughts produce an effect upon the body, and this in turn affects everything it comes in contact with. Low and grovelling thoughts, or pure and noble thoughts, leave their image stamped indelibly upon the features, and even change the general shape of the body. So that the body is a kind of photographic plate of the mind.

2. If this is true of our body, it is especially so of the mind. That is more pliable than any wax cylinder, and far more sensitive than any photographic plate. There is an often quoted incident, commented on by Coleridge, of the servant-maid of a German professor, who, while ill of fever, repeated long phrases of Greek and Hebrew, having by chance, when well, heard her master utter them aloud. We speak of an impression being made on the mind, and it is no doubt so; but that is just what is true of the wax cylinder by the needle. So men and women have vividly brought back in a moment scenes, words, and acts of their childhood. In some emergency, when the phonograph is turned rapidly for only a moment, whole scenes in the past life are brought out.

We, and the whole universe about us, are like one endless mass of gelatine, to be touched and permanently affected by our every act, word, look, or thought. Think, then, of the possible witnesses God can have of our lives in the Judgment! Joshua's stone was only one of the numerous witnesses God could call upon as to Israel's faithfulness.

We ourselves will be phonographic cylinders, and photographic plates, and will forever see and read our past. This is a book God will open to our eyes and ears. We will also read the impress we have made on others. Behold, then, the good and the terrible in this! Joy at seeing our kind acts, and hearing our loving words, and the awfulness of having all our evil brought out again!

But all wax cylinders with bad messages, and photographic plates with dark pictures, can be laid aside, shelved, covered by the death of Christ, never to be read, revealed, nor mentioned. "All his transgressions that he hath committed, they shall not be mentioned unto him."

VI.

CARBON.

That which is born of the flesh is flesh; and that which is born of the Spirit is spirit. John 3:6.

[OBJECTS.—The diamond, the graphite (a large stick of the solid material), charcoal, anthracite coal, gas-carbon, and lampblack; a lamp, or, better, a Bunsen burner. All these things differ, and yet they are the same, for they are composed of one and the same element, carbon. They do not look alike, but they are composed of only one thing, carbon. The lampblack is a soft, dust-like material which is so inflammable that it often takes fire spontaneously in the air; while the diamond is the hardest of materials and so extremely incombustible that it is difficult to burn it even in oxygen gas. Nothing is in one of these things that is not in all the others. The great difference is explained by the difference in the grouping or arranging of the elementary atoms.]

I. Notice the looks and history of each one of these. They are all alike in many things.

  1. When they are first discovered or brought

to notice, they usually are very unpromising in looks. This is especially true of all but the diamond, and is often true of that.

2. They all have value; diamonds because of their rarity and beauty.

3. They have been brought up out of the earth or some dark or muddy place.

4. Usually, when handled, they soil the hands, leaving them black and smutty.

5. They were all once in a very different form than they are at present. Some were trees or vegetables, and it is generally thought that all of them were. So they have met with a fall. They no doubt once existed in the gaseous state.

6. If they were originally a vegetable product, then they have treasured up in them that which has been given them from the air, and sun—another world.

7. Apply heat, and light is the result. (Hold them in the flame.)

8. They then give forth heat themselves. (Prominently true of coal.)

9. When heat is applied to them, they give out light and heat, and are at the same time changed into an invisible gas, and a small amount of ashes or waste material.

These things represent all men by nature. They look very different, but "there is no difference." They have this one thing in common: a fallen nature, which is a fleshly nature. Men may be low down in sin, like the lampblack. Others may have a life that looks very beautiful, and is very rare, and yet they are of the flesh—they have the carbon or lampblack nature. The atoms of the fleshly nature may be grouped or arranged in a great variety of ways, and thus change the appearance; but still it is true that "that which is born of the flesh is flesh."

II. Notice how like these various forms of carbon, the sinner is by nature.

1. Unpromising at the first. What is more so than a rebellious child of God?

2. Value. What God has paid for the sinner shows his value.

3. When brought into service, they are brought up out of darkness; a horrible pit of miry clay.

4. Contact with sinful persons soils. The black will rub off.

5. The original state was very different; they fell.

6. They have treasured up within them a remnant of the Divine Nature, the image that came from another world.

7. Apply the Holy Spirit, Who is the divine light and fire, and they give forth light. Through the power of the Holy Spirit, sinners are made the light of the world.

8. Through this heat which is imparted to them, they throw out heat to warm others.

9. In coming in contact with this Fire, they are changed from flesh to spirit. *a.* Get into this Flame. *b.* The change takes place at once, and yet it is more or less of a continuous process. Some require a longer holding in the fire than others, to be changed entirely into the invisible. *c.* So hold still in this Fire. *d.* The fire searches and tries every part, and so it is a consuming process. *e.* Give the fire a good chance, and there will be nothing left of the coal but a little ashes. All the rest will be gas. Give the Holy Spirit a chance at the old nature, and soon it will be consumed, and in its stead there will be spirit. That born of the Spirit, will be spirit. All that will be left of the sinner who remains in this Fire will be the ashes of the old nature, and spirit will be in its place.

The one indispensable thing every unconverted person needs is this Divine Fire. The one indispensable thing every Christian needs is the baptism, and that continuously, of the Holy Ghost, and of fire. The first, that he may have imparted unto him the light of life, and the second, that he may have imparted unto him the fire of death, that the old nature may be consumed. Both are necessary, for "That which is born of the flesh is flesh; and that which is born of the Spirit is spirit."

VII.

THE LIFE THAT WILL STAND.

The ungodly shall not stand in the judgment. Ps. 1:5.
So stand fast in the Lord. Phil. 4:1.

[OBJECTS.—Ten blocks of wood three by four inches in size, the shortest one ten inches long, and the others gradually increasing in length till the last one is about two feet. Have the three-inch face of each painted white. Then beginning with No. 1, which is the shortest, paint in large black letters with lampblack and turpentine, "More"; 2, "Covets"; 3, "Lying"; 4. "Stealing"; 5, "Irreverence"; 6, "Drinking"; 7, "Self-reform"; 8.

"Good Deeds"; 9, "Self-righteous"; 10, "Deceived." A box which is a perfect cube, about a foot each way, with a lid that can be locked. Paint it white, and print in large red letters "Faith," on two opposite faces, "Hope" on two other opposite faces, and "Love" on the two other faces. Put a Bible in it and lock it. Have all these things concealed, and brought out, and used only as fast as needed.]

I. What we wish to represent is the character of an unconverted person from the beginning to the end of life. Every such life is made up of certain points, or traits of character.

1. One of the first things in which a child shows that it has a fallen nature, is its desire for more. We will stand this block with "More" printed on it, to represent this trait in the child's character. It is one of the first stakes that is set when the child begins to assert himself. He wants more than he has, he is dissatisfied with his toys, his knife, his books, his kite, his food, his clothes, the small amount of money he has, or something. This spirit of discontent which begins to be seen in boys and girls never leaves them. It follows them down to old age, and to the grave. If it is well directed, under the influence of God's grace, then well; if it is left to grow in its own

way, then ill, for it leads the fallen nature on to one other stake in the character.

2. The child wants more, and then he covets that which is another's. This, you see, is a little higher than the other.

It makes the character a little more unstable than before. The child covets the playthings of another when young, and when old he covets the possessions of others, whether they are great or small. There is no sin that this will not lead to.

3. Then comes lying. This is one of the products of covetousness. A child wants more than he has, and he lies to get it. It may be small or it may be large, but the lie is a lie whether over a small, or a large thing. One lie is told, and then another has to be told to conceal the first, and so lies keep on growing; and when one is discovered, they all fall together, and the reputation of the one who told them, for now he is a liar. That stake is set in the nature never to be fully torn out, except by divine grace, and often after that comes into the heart, there are slivers of that old stick left in the soil, to disgrace the Christian and his Master too. It is astonishing how many will tell lies. With many, it is so much a habit that they think little of it; and they just as little realize that they usually fail to deceive, because they are not aware that others

know their sin. People soon learn to estimate the statements of those who are not very particular what they say. Too much cannot be said against this sin, for it is one of the long black marks which shows the fallen nature.

4. In close fellowship with lying is stealing. One who misrepresents in business, to gain a point, will soon take, to gain a point. The spirit to steal began with Adam and Eve. They stole the forbidden fruit, and fruit growers and venders have had to suffer loss from little and big Adams and Eves ever since. It would be fortunate if this spirit would only stop with fruit, but it does not. It extends to everything in life. Those with this spirit steal the property, the business, the families, the love, and even the good name of others. They do not stop here, but go on and steal even from God. "Will a man rob God?" Yes, they rob Him of His good name, of His children, of the service that belongs to Him, of His tithes and His Sabbaths. The thieving spirit in the nature is a longer and blacker stake than any yet, and it makes the life more insecure than ever.

5. This sin against man and God leads to another, irreverence. Those who lie and steal have little respect for God, or His interests. And irreverence leads to rebellion, which is the spirit that Satan has toward God. Look

out for irreverence, for it will show itself all the way from inattention while God is being addressed in prayer, to bold defiance of His will and power. We will put this block in line with the others, as another bad mark in the unconverted person's life.

6. Another mark of many an unchristian life is drinking, or some such sin. Whether this be indulged in little or much, it is one more thing to weaken the character. This block represents those who live to gratify their desires. It may be in eating or drinking, in opium or morphine taking. These are the sins of the flesh. The flesh rises up, and is the master of the soul. The spirit becomes such a slave to these lusts of the flesh, that the very mention of these sins to the one guilty of them, causes him to rise in anger in their defence. But this is another manifestation of the sinful nature, and we will stand it here, so that all these weak things may be seen together as prominent points of the character, which we often look upon as small and unimportant, while God sees them to be large and hideous.

7. As we now stand and look at these blocks, and think of them as representing the character of any one person, we cannot help saying, "What a row of hideous traits to be in any one character!" There is need of any one like this to call a halt, and especially if the sins are

known to mortal eye. So we will stand up one more trait of this fallen nature, which is "self-reformation." A new leaf is turned. It is a real leaf, for many of the worst sins are at once stopped. Everything that could offend the taste of man is laid aside.

8. Now good deeds must be brought into the line. They flow out abundantly. Lying, stealing, slandering, and all abuse of others are put aside. He is kind to the poor, and exceedingly so. He meets all his obligations promptly. He has no spot in his life now, that men can put their finger on. So he thinks that this is a great addition to his character.

9. But no one can have such a life and not value it. He does most certainly, and if it were possible he would take it, and stand it out one side and say, "See that life, will you!" So he needs nothing better, he thinks, than this good life of his. He trusts it to bring him out right in the eyes of men, and also with God. So we will have to erect another little monument to represent an element in this character, and this one is "Self-righteousness." This is a very tall trait of many a character, and it overshadows and overtops every other trait except the last, which is:

10. "Deception." The soul is deceived. How many monuments there would be raised, if there were one for each person who is de-

ceived! Every one of these sins has been leading on to this one dangerous state of the soul. It stands up above all other traits, and is the last one. With this one the life is ended. The soul with all these points in his character, however little or much they may have been developed, is about to pass into eternity, to appear before the One Who is to judge all, and Who has known all from the first. How will this life stand before the Judge? The first text in Ps. 1 tells us, "The ungodly shall not stand in the judgment." One breath from the Almighty will cause all such deception as this to fall; and what an awful fall it will be! The scales drop from the eyes, and with that down goes all the life together, and with a mighty crash, the sound of which will ring in the ears of the lost one forever. (Blow upon the last one, and it falls against the one next to it, and they all fall together.)

II. The Christian life is represented by very different characteristics than these, and it ends very differently. This cube more properly represents his life. As on it are printed "Faith," "Hope," and "Love," so the true Christian has first of all faith in Christ. He trusts Him alone to be saved from sin here, and from the judgment hereafter. So through every trial, he has a big hope in God for this world, and for that which is to come. He has also love to God and man. Now set him down and look at him. You see he is just as big one way as he is another. He has his trials, just as well as any other person, and sometimes he seems to have more than others. But notice what they do with him. Some great trial comes to him, and it seems to overwhelm him. Over he appears, to human eyes, to go, but, lo! he is just as tall as ever. And you may knock him over with trials and abuses and slanders and bereavements till, like Job, he has nothing apparently left, and still he is as much right side up as ever. Even martyrdom cannot cause him to fall. It is true, his faith, hope, and love look larger at some times than at others. But he always has some in view. (The letters on the box should be longer on some sides than others, to represent this.)

The reason for this is apparent. He has a door, before which One has stood and knocked. This door has been unlocked, the bolt has been thrown back (unlock the door of the box), and a power has entered, that was stronger than the one that reigned there. (Here take out the Bible.) The living Word of God has been received within, and it has made the dead soul alive. It is the *logos* of God, the Word which is spirit and life to the soul that has Him within, and which makes it alive. As he has Christ within him, he can fulfil the injunction in the text in Phil. 4:1. He stands fast in the Lord. Like the Psalmist, he says, "Thy word have I hid in my heart, that I might not sin against thee." This life within is a hidden life, and it will be brought fully to light when the door is unlocked in the great testing day. It is manifest without, in a pure life, represented by the white, and always shows faith, hope, and love. This is the only life that will stand the test of the Judgment Day. "The ungodly shall not stand in the judgment," "So stand fast in the Lord," that you may be among those who shall stand in that day.

VIII.

Lessons from a Frog.

[Object.—A live frog if possible; if not, a Japanese imitation from the stores. Let it sit on the floor by your feet as you talk about it.]

I. There is a great change which the frog meets with in its life. This is its anomaly. At one time it is a tadpole, and it changes into the frog, a most wonderful change.

This is like the change in man from spiritual death to spiritual life. The person is the same, and yet so different. This change differs from that which the frog undergoes in that it is an entirely new life, while with the frog it is only a change of the old nature.

II. The tadpole stage of life is all lived under water, while during the frog life the little animal remains only a little while at a time under the water.

So the unconverted one lives only in this world. That is his element. He cannot live in any other element till he is changed. When a boy, I used to catch the little tadpoles in the ponds, but they could not live out of the water. So the soul is out of its element when among Christians, till it is regenerated.

The Christian is very different from this. He can live for only a short time in the element of this world. His business leads him to dive down into the world, but he has to come up often, in order to get some fresh air from Heaven.

Some Christians stay so long under water without breathing that they very nearly, if not quite, lose their life. Prayer, communion with God, is the Christian's vital breath. If you need to go down into the world occasionally, do not forget to come up often to breathe. Do not catch hold of some root or stone down there, and remain there. That means suffocation.

III. In passing from the tadpole stage to the frog, the tadpole loses the hard, bony part of its mouth. It is an essential in the change of its life.

So all true Christians, in passing from the lower to the higher life, lose the hard part of that organ that James says in his Epistle has never been tamed.

The tadpole's mouth is changed. Even in its bony state it can do comparatively little harm to the animal world. This is very different from the great harm that can be done by the mouth that is not controlled by the bit and bridle of God's grace. And how much grace it often requires to change this little organ!

IV. Frogs have suffered greatly because of their resemblance to toads. This resemblance is often close, to the unskilled eye. Indeed, many persons do not know the difference.

So many are unable to distinguish a Christian from one who is not. The resemblance is often very close. The unchristian and the Christian have so many things in common, just as the frog and the toad have, that they are often mistaken the one for the other. Yet there is of necessity a vital difference between their lives, in belief, conduct, and habits. Any skilful eye can generally detect the difference. It is a shame that there is often so little difference in appearance.

V. You cannot judge by the looks of the frog how far he can leap. We are too liable, even with a frog, to judge all by outward appearances. Fine dress, culture, money, social standing, and many other things often lead us to judge falsely in regard to one's character. The Scripture tells us to judge nothing from appearance, an admonition which young people would do well to heed in forming friendships and associations, perhaps for life.

VI. Examine these little animals closely, and you will see that they have a beautiful eye. Conscience, the eye of the soul, how beautiful it is if it is not put out, or dimmed by sin!

VII. They have their enemies. Men often like to eat them. They lie in wait for them long, and exult over them when at last the little fellows lie helpless on the table, furnishing them a dainty dish.

So Satan, our enemy, would swallow us quick. Our other enemies nibble off a little here, and a little there, and would destroy us by a little bite at a time. But Satan lies about fishing for our soul. He leads us on by one bait and another, until at last he would make an end of us quick, through suicide, or murder as a result of bad company. We must not be ignorant of his devices.

VIII. These little animals differ from many quadrupeds, in having the gift of voice, and they know how to use it too. In the old feudal days they used to congregate in great numbers in the ditches, or moats, which were left half full of water about castles. The serfs and vassals were kept splashing the water night and morning to keep the frogs from singing, so that the lords could sleep.

So Christians are blessed with a voice, and should use it too. Let the enemy splash to keep you silent; you keep lost and sleeping souls awake. Be sure to be heard in line of work. Make it as hard as possible for lost ones to continue in their sleep of death. Let the world know that you are alive from the dead.

IX. The frog, though small and counted of very little importance, is useful. He keeps bugs and worms from plants and bushes.

You may be a "worm and no man," yet God can use a worm, if it is willing to be a worm, and to be used. Are you willing to do a little work? A frog cannot make a rose-bush, but he may save its life by destroying the insects that would soon kill it. You cannot create an angel or a soul, but you can save that soul from utter ruin by killing the little insects of doubt, fear, rebellion against Christ, and the like, which have lodged upon the soul.

You have your work, as well as the frog, and are no less important to the spiritual world than the frog is to the plant world.

X. The stormy fall soon comes, and the frogs go and bury themselves deep in the mud. Often they go in troops. There they lie dormant and unconscious in the cold frozen ground. If you should find one, you could break it in pieces, as it would have no feeling.

So the stormy fall is coming to you. You will soon be buried, for the summer of this life is passing. Death is coming. Are you living your life well now?

XI. But the spring comes; then the frogs seem to have a new life, and come forth to see the beautiful flowers, and thrive in the ponds that have been made warm by the sunshine.

How like the resurrection morning is this! Death comes, yet it is not death, for the morning cometh. "We shall not all sleep." Some shall be awake. Others are only sleeping till that spring-time day shall come. What a day and what changes will be wrought upon it! It will not be like the passing of a winter night for the frog, and the coming of the spring. The frog only comes back to his old life again, while the Christain passes on through death, and emerges on the other side in a much more perfect and glorious life, and to live in a new and infinitely more glorious world. The mortal puts on immortality.

Are you of no account? Go and consider the poor frog. He lies asleep now deep in the mud. Has God made him of some importance, and given him a mission, and not you?

Have you met with the great change, and are you being useful, just to stop death's work on some rose-bush in God's garden?

IX.

THE OLD DRY BONES.

The hand of the Lord was upon me, and carried me out in the spirit of the Lord, and set me down in the midst of the valley which was full of bones, etc. Ezek. 37: 1 10.

[OBJECTS.—A lot of dry bones, collected from a market or restaurant. The greater the variety in shapes and sizes the better.

Give a vivid description of what you see as you go with Ezekiel into the valley of dry bones. Display the bones collected.]

There are some things in which these bones, and those Ezekiel saw are alike: 1. Once they had life. 2. They are dry, showing that they have been dead a long time. 3. They are in a confused state, and were originally from widely different regions. Perhaps some of these here came from Texas, some from Michigan, and some from New York State. So in that valley of dry bones, they were of different persons, families, and possibly of different regions. 4. But a worse state of decay awaits them. 5. They have a very dark outlook. They have no hope, unless miraculous power be exerted upon them.

There are some important ways in which these bones, and those in that valley differ: 1. The bones Ezekiel saw are spoken of as having the power of hearing. 2. A promise is made to them. 3. Divine power comes upon them, and there is (*a*) a noise, (*b*) a shaking, and (*c*) a coming into order. 4. A breath is breathed upon them, and there result life, vigor, and beauty.

The dry bones in the valley have a fourfold reference.

I. To Israel. Nationally and religiously, they were like these dry bones. They had neither life nor unity as a nation, and spiritually they were as dead.

II. They represent a frequent state of the church of Christ. The death that reigned in that valley, and that reigns among these bones, is like the death in the church before the Reformation in the sixteenth century. Such too, is the lamentable condition of many a church at the present day.

III. Here is a reference to the resurrection of the dead: "For the hour is coming in the which all that are in their graves shall hear His voice, and shall come forth."

IV. In these bones there is also a reference to the individual soul that is in a state of sin.

1. As this pile of bones, and those that Ezekiel saw, once had life, so in the soul of man there was once a divine life that has long since departed. Look at these bones! They once had life. So you can go through a museum and look at the dried mummies, and say to yourself: "These have barely the form now. They once walked and talked, lived and loved, like me." In a like manner God looks on the souls of men. Once they were alive like Him, and together the creature and Creator talked and walked in the Garden in the cool of the day. It is a sad thing to think what the soul once was, and the great change in it. As you go through the old castle at Heidelberg the guide says to you, "Here is where Luther stayed when he visited here"; in such a room a certain prince is said to have been entertained. You see here and there remains of the beauty of architecture, and you exclaim, "How grand this must have been once!" But what a change! There lies a large part of that once magnificent tower; an enemy in time of war did that work of destruction! See too how

the elements and neglect have done their work of destruction!

See the destruction wrought by the enemy of souls, in Africa and China! It is much like the ruin of the great cities of the Orient. Just as those ancient cities, mounds, and ruins are explored and unearthed, and, through the skill of the archæologist, one can see something of what they must have been at one time, so civilization is an attempt at unearthing, and education, a restoration of the soul to its original design and beauty. They fail utterly, except in giving us a little idea of the grandeur of the soul before its ruin.

2. These are dry bones, indicating that they have been a long time dead. They are not annihilated, but the spirit has gone out of them. The soul of every unconverted person is like them. It is not annihilated; it has an existence, but it is dead. A watch with no mainspring in it is a dead watch, yet it is not annihilated. So the soul is dead to God; it lacks the mainspring—the Spirit of God.

3. These bones are a confused mass, they are in disorder. The soul that is in sin, is more like these bones than it is like the orderly arrangement in the watch with no mainspring. In every unconverted soul there is disorder. The powers of the man are not working in harmony one with the other.

4. But a worse state than this is in store for them, if they continue as they are. This world may be bad, it often is a hard place in which to live; but the one who commits suicide does not better his state. He only goes to a worse life. It can be worse than it is, even to the one who is suffering, and it certainly will be to those who continue in sin.

5. There is a hopeless outlook for these bones, as far as man's aid is concerned. I can walk up to these bones and say, "O bones! I will now undertake your case," and, if they had the power of hearing, the only consolation they might have, would be that I caused them to hope, and had thus deceived them. Just so much, and no more, is any soul benefited when any minister or priest undertakes its case. It may be deceived, but it cannot be made alive. A drunkard cried out in his despair to me recently, "I say my prayers and go to confession, and all this seems to make no difference with me." So it is ever, unless it results in deception of the soul, which is a worse state than before. All these things are like Gehazi's staff laid on the face of the dead child: there is neither voice nor hearing, for there is no life. And a man's own efforts at self-reformation, are just as fruitless as would be the efforts of these bones at self-resurrection.

V. There are some differences between these bones and those that Ezekiel saw.

1. Those he saw had the power of hearing. So the soul of the sinner hears, but it is the hearing of one having the nightmare. He seems to hear and see, but cannot move hand or foot, or utter a cry for help, till the spell is broken. So Satan has thrown a spell around the soul, and keeps it a prisoner.

2. The promise comes, "Ye shall live." "The dead shall hear the voice of the Son of God: and they that hear shall live." Here is the only hope of the soul, and it is a big one if embraced.

3. The divine word is uttered to these bones, and there is a noise, a shaking, and a coming together. So God speaks to the heart by His providence, possibly by a death as He spoke to Luther. He speaks by His Holy Spirit, and the soul is thrown into confusion. A noise is heard in the dead regions of the soul. Sometimes the one spoken to rushes madly on into the valley of death. He often seems to be going swiftly to destruction.

There is also a shaking of every prop under the soul; every part is tried to its utmost. The Spirit of God touching the sinner is something like a powerful galvanic battery touching a dead body. There is a wonderful shaking. Some are so mightily stirred to the very depths of their souls, that they are not able to eat or sleep for days. This was the case of C. G. Finney, and of many others.

Then there is a coming together. Order comes out of confusion. Sins are laid aside. The right way to God is asked for earnestly, as the exiled Jews must have come together, and consulted as to the possibility of their return home. Works are done meet for repentance. Any soul seeing his state as it is before God, will stop every sin he knows of, if it is possible. But this is not enough. There may be order and not life, and just here lies the danger. These bones might come into order, and form a perfect skeleton, like the little one I hold in my hand, but that is all fruitless as long as there is not life. The danger in this age is that dead souls that are shaken by the Spirit, will be aroused into a reformed life and clothe themselves with respectable conduct, join the church, and let the matter rest, and it is a rest of death. Without doubt—and it is a lamentable fact—there are tens of thousands of skeletons in the churches, who are robed in the garments of decency, but in whom there is not one spark of divine life.

4. So the breath of the Almighty is needed. When Adam was perfectly formed, he yet needed one thing, and that was life. God breathed into his nostrils, and he became a

living soul. By his sin he became a dead soul—the Spirit of life departed from him. Man needs that same breath of God to come within him again, that he may live to God. This is no doubt the meaning of God in this parable shown to Ezekiel. God's breath must be breathed into the dead before it can live. And this is one thing that every soul must have, or remain dead forever; the "*pneuma*" or Spirit of God, must come within him. Then there is life, eternal life. There is also vigor, which is the activity of that life. There is beauty, for the beauty of the Author must be mirrored in that life. But these come only in the order named, everlasting life, undying vigor, and never-fading beauty. What a wonderful transformation is this from the dead, dry bones!

X.

The Striking Contrast Between the Bread of the Devil and the Bread of the Lord Illustrated.

Wherefore do ye spend money for that which is not bread? and your labor for that which satisfieth not? hearken diligently unto me, and eat ye that which is good, and let your soul delight itself in fatness. Isa. 55: 2.

[OBJECTS.—A table on the left, with no cloth, and having on it some husks mentioned in the parable of the prodigal son, and some lentils, for which Esau bargained (these can be bought at nearly any fruit stand or grocer's), an old bottle with a few drops of some dark fluid, a dish of ashes, or anything that makes this table uninviting, as far as the hope of getting any food is concerned. Cover all with a black cloth until it is desired. On the right, have a table very neatly spread with several luxuries and dainties for food. One table represents the Devil's fare, and the other Christ's. Have card-boards for the first table, to be used as wanted, with the following words printed in large letters, which can be read across the church: "No Bread; Much Money; Hard Labor; No Satisfaction." The cards for the second table have printed on them: "No Money; No Labor; A Good Ear; Good Food; Great Delight." These are the points for each table. Uncover the first table, and call attention to it, and place the cards on it in view, one after the other. Follow up with the second, sitting down and having something to eat, if you care to do so.]

The soul of man is full of longings and desires, aspirations and needs. There are various ways of satisfying these.

I. By eating at the Devil's table. The prodigal did this. The bill of fare is:

1. *No bread.* "Is not bread." Greely and his men in their Arctic exploration were so reduced, that they had to boil their fur coats, and boots for food. So Satan feeds the souls who depend upon him. The black soup in prison fare, is a type of the Devil's soup. He gives not a crust of food. An impoverished system, constantly growing weaker and weaker, is the result of feeding on his fare. Blood-poisoning is another result. At last the blood is tainted with all manner of evil.

Every one eats at the Devil's table who gives himself to sinning. There is no state of corruption in the world that is not caused by this; yet it gives not one mouthful of bread.

2. "Much money" is one other thing in the bill of fare. (Exhibit the card, "Much Money," and put it on the table.) The Devil stands like one of the dumb clerks in the railway stations offering its wares. "Drop in your nickel, pull the handle, and out will come your fortune." The first you find truly easy, the second you work long at, and the third you fail in, with all of Satan's machines.

See the fortunes of money spent at the Devil's table, the drinking saloon. Does this give any benefit? Are those who drink any better off than those who do not? Seventy-five million dollars in New York City go from the pockets, mainly, of the poor and laboring people to furnish this bill of fare at the Devil's table.

See how men weigh out their money in gambling. Are they better for all this outlay? How much is spent for lust! How much for the bubbles of pleasure!

The arch-fiend stands by all the cess-pools of sin, and says: "Drop in the nickels, away from your wife and children, yourself and your home, and see some coveted sin pop out." And on swell the crowds, and in drop the pennies, and out pop the pails of beer, or the like, and each one goes on with his fortune.

3. "Hard Labor" is the next thing on this table. What a vast amount of labor has been expended by man to try to satisfy the soul-thirst with something that is not bread. Think of the Colosseum of Vespasian and Titus, which could seat 87,000 persons, and accommodate 15,000 more spectators, where 5,000 beasts are said to have been slaughtered in one hundred days, and many human lives sacrificed; and all this labor was done, and these cruel and bloody shows were given, to satisfy the cravings of the soul for bread.

How men labor for money to satisfy their hunger. Matthew Hale Smith says: "No artisan, no laborer, in any machine shop or factory in the land toils so much like a galley slave as our richest men who are in business. There isn't a man in the country, who has the ability, who would do the work that William B. Astor does daily, for ten thousand dollars a year. His office resembles a police prison, and here he works, rarely taking exercise, and toiling on, early and late, and tramping on foot from his home to his office and back."

How many anxious hours and what unceasing toil Napoleon spent for his passing glory! I know a woman who bent over her work from daylight till dark, while she was young, for fear she would die in the poor-house. Now she is old, and she is more bent over it than ever, a slave to the miserly desire for gain.

The Michigan lumbermen, while up in their camps in the woods, do not see their camps by daylight, they go out into the woods to work so early and return so late; and yet all the money is gone in a week or two, when they get down into the towns, among the saloons. All this hard labor to satisfy the spirit's craving with something that is not bread, and that for only a few days!

Those who eat at the Devil's table must work in his tread-mill, something as men keep the horse climbing up the endless horse-powers, when they saw wood or thresh grain in the country. They keep climbing, and work exceedingly hard at it, but they make no advance.

Very few men in the world reach the plane they are aiming for, and even then they keep in the tread-mill, but the millions of others do not reach any great eminence, and you and I are among the latter multitudes, and not the very few. Like the horse in the power, we may think we shall reach the top, but it will probably be with us about as it is now, and then will come death. So, labor not for that which is not bread.

4. "No Satisfaction" is the last thing in the bill of fare at this table. All from this table to satisfy hunger are like the salt water of the sea to quench thirst—it only increases the desire without satisfying the thirst in the least. "Alexander conquered the world, yet that could not satisfy his soul. If he could have conquered all the worlds that stud the heavens, he would have wept for more." "All the rivers run into the sea; yet the sea is not full." "The eye is not satisfied with seeing, nor the ear filled with hearing." So the desire for riches, honor, glory, and pleasures are never satisfied, for there is in the soul a vacancy the world can never fill. The Christian's "cup runneth over," but God never made a soul so small, and poor, and mean that the whole universe could fill its needs.

II. God's table is very different from the one we have been considering.

1. The first thing about this is, you come to it with "no money, and no labor." The best things of God cannot be bought; the air, the sunshine, the rain, life, and health cannot be gotten in any other way than received. This is true also of the blessings for the soul: they may be received, but cannot be had for money or labor.

2. In coming to this table one needs only "a good ear." A good ear is an open ear. Many have ears, but they are stopped up with something, such as future hopes, present lusts, past sins that they will hold on to, and pride that they are not willing to bring down. An open ear is an attentive, eager, listening ear; it is an ear which gets *down*, something as the Indians put their ear down to the earth, to listen to the coming of a friend or foe, or as one puts his ear down on the railway track and hears the coming of the train, even before it is in sight. Our stiff necks must bend to get our ears down very low.

A good ear is such an ear as the inhabitants of Samaria had when the lepers came from the camp of the Syrians and shouted up to those on the wall, " BREAD! " Such an ear always leads to bread. It did them, and certainly does lead to Christ the living bread. A diligent hearkening never fails to bring the hungry soul a feast.

3. "Good food" is always on this table. It is good, for it gives life at the touch. As the dead man revived, and stood upon his feet, when he touched the bones of Elisha, so life comes into the dead soul, and he revives and stands upon his feet when he comes in contact with Christ, the bread of life. One touch of the soul by the Living Spirit of Christ means life.

It is good food, because it nourishes. It so nourishes the soul that it makes wonderful strides in its growth while feeding on only this. What a terrible thing to be a babe forever, always weak, yet alive! See how it made Peter grow from the weak, timid, denying disciple to the bold martyr for Christ. If you are only a babe, and that continually, it is because you do not eat enough of God's food —you do not take in enough of the living Christ.

It is good food, for it is wonderfully strengthening. This is what took Christ through His forty days' fast and conflict with the Devil. So, it took Job through his trials, temptations, and afflictions; and so has it taken some of you here through many mighty conflicts and fiery trials, till you have been surprised at your strength. But it was not yours, it was God's, which you received by feeding on Him. His food, the Holy Spirit, will take a person through anything. Sometimes the blows fall thick and fast, and with mighty force, as they fell upon Christ in Pilate's hall, and upon Paul and Silas before they were dragged into the Ephesian jail. But a little of the strength that is "made perfect in weakness," so girds the soul with might that it can endure all these things, and call them "light afflictions."

This is good food, because it is so easily digested; it fits every part of the nature. Health books make out lists of articles of food, and the time it takes the stomach to digest them. That is the best food which affords the most nourishment, and can be digested in the shortest time. The food God gives the soul, affords eternal nourishment — eternal life — eternal growth, and instantaneous assimilation.

4. There is "great delight" in partaking of this table. Food may be ever so good, and nourishing, but if one is a dyspeptic he can have no delight in eating.

The food that Christ gives is delightful, because it satisfies the longings of the soul for certainty about the other world.

It satisfies the felt need of a personal leader, one to look up to, one who knows how to guide, one able to lead to victory, one to tell every trouble to, which we feel we must tell to some one; the soul cries for this, one whom we can always love and trust.

"One of Trench's poems, 'The Monk and the Bird,' is the story of a monk who feared lest he should in Heaven grow weary with the monotony of goodness and worship. One day, wandering in the woods, he heard a bird singing very charmingly, and stopped to listen, as he thought, for a short hour. But on returning to the convent he found that he had listened two whole generations, and all the monks were now perfect strangers to him." So great is the delight of the heart that communes with God, that a thousand years will be as one day in heaven, and an earnest of that life is the Holy Spirit in the heart here.

But you must eat, or all this will do you no good.

XI.

The Electric Indicator.

Therefore, as by the offence of one, judgment came upon all men to condemnation; even so by the righteousness of one the free gift came upon all men unto justification of life. Rom. 5 : 18.

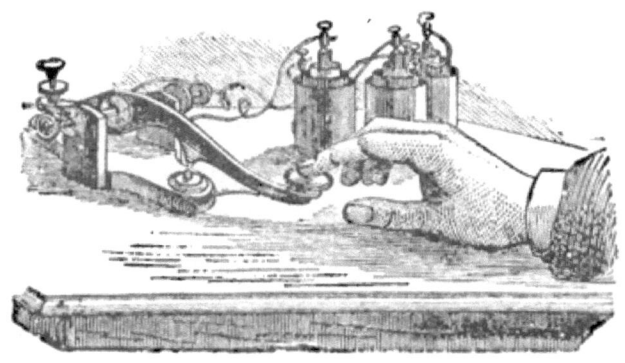

[OBJECT.—An electric indicator with batteries, and a wire running up to the top of the building, and back to the machine. The machine can thus be used.]

Through his sin, man was cut off from God, the source of his spiritual life. So by the righteousness of one man has he the possibility of being again joined to God.

This machine represents the human being.

I. Alone it is useless and powerless. It

must be connected with the wires, and so to the battery. So of the soul. It must be connected to God. The at-one-ment or atonement has been made by Christ.

II. The wires are *dead*, and the machine dead, till the electric current gets into them.

So the atonement is useless till the Holy Spirit applies it to the soul. Those dead in sins must be touched by the living power before they can live. The living current is all at hand to be used.

III. Before the current can be used, the key must be pushed down.

So the key of man's soul, the will, must be touched and brought into subjection to the will of God before the power can flow into the soul. The wires will be connected, and charged in vain, if this is not done. God's demand that the will yield to Him before salvation is granted, is not an arbitrary thing, any more than it is that the key be pressed to allow the flow of the electric current. One is as much a necessity as the other.

IV. The more resistance, and the more electric power is put on, the more certainly will the machine be ruined. A great amount of electricity, and great resistance set buildings on fire. Some electric currents are so powerful, and there is so much resistance in the electric machine, that the latter is burned out.

The more resistance the sinner offers to God, and the more the Holy Spirit strives, the more certainly and swiftly will the soul be ruined.

V. As I touch the key, the response comes immediately. Yield to Christ with all your heart, and salvation comes at once. It is something like sending a cablegram across from England. The reply is dated so that it seems to be answered before the message is sent by you. So God answers before the words leave the lips—the very moment the heart yields.

VI. Both arms must be holding the wires, and they must be insulated. These are necessities. So you must take hold of Christ with both hands, and be insulated by the Holy Spirit's presence from sinful contact with the world. These are necessities also.

VII. There is no use in ticking away, if there is no connection. Human efforts at salvation are entirely fruitless, except in deluding the soul. If our neighbor's machine is all out of repair, it will not mend our own. If another is lost, it will not save me.

VIII. The longer the machine is unused, and the more it is used for other purposes than that for which it was intended, the less likely it is to work. Dig in the ground with it, and you will soon ruin it completely.

Man's soul was made to love and worship

God. If it is left to run to waste, or used to grovel in the service of Satan, it will soon be ruined beyond all repair. The Spirit's power may be waiting to be used to give life, while the soul is putting itself beyond His power to save. There is life only in being joined to Christ by the Holy Spirit.

XII.

OUR BROKEN PLANK.

The way of life is above to the wise, that he may depart from hell beneath. Prov. 15:24.

[OBJECT.—A rough sketch of a plank stretching from one precipice to another, over a bottomless chasm. The plank is broken because of a great stone on its centre.]

Life is a road or way. We are all in the way and on the way. This plank represents our moral life, which extends from this world on into the next. On this plank every one walks for a longer or shorter time in this journey of life. Some never depend upon anything else to take them safely over to the other world.

I. Every one's plank is broken, and sin has done it. Ecc. 7:20: "For there is not a just man upon earth, that doeth good, and sinneth not." Prov. 20:9: "Who can say, I have made my heart clean, I am pure from my sin?" Rom. 3:22, 23: "For there is no difference: For all have sinned, and come short of the glory of God." So this fact excludes all boasting.

II. Notice the manner in which some planks are broken. Start out the first man, Adam. His plank breaks. It was his stomach that caused his fall, and it has caused many to fall since. Let another walk on the plank, Noah. Drink is his fall and disgrace. With Moses, the meek man, it is his temper: he becomes angry, and breaks the tables of the law. A hasty temper has made many a man, and sometimes a woman, break the law since. David falls under the power of lust, which began with evil thoughts. Saul's plank breaks under the weight of pride and jealousy. March Israel, in the wilderness of Sin, on the plank. How plank after plank gives way under the one sin, unbelief! With Judas and Achan it was covetousness, and with Peter it was his self-confidence. Fall after fall has been taking place ever since these fell, and still the falls go on. No living person can say he has not fallen. Only one has ever crossed without his moral life breaking in a single place, and that is the Son of God.

III. The result of this fall is to sink into the bottomless pit below. If one were falling, and he were asleep, he would not know he was falling. Perhaps he might be dreaming that he was sitting safely upon a rock. If one were on a sinking ship, and was dreaming of his safety, it would by no means make him safe. All are falling over the pit. Some are asleep, dreaming. God calls, "Awake, thou that sleepest, and arise from the dead."

Some know they are falling, and call upon God, and the hand from above catches hold of them, as Jesus caught hold of sinking Peter. Those who thus cry are the wise ones of the text. *Christ* is the hand that catches them. All fall, but there is a great difference between continuing to fall, and being *caught*. A child who falls from the window of a high building, and is caught, may not be much injured by the fall, and is much safer in his rescuer's arms than he was before.

Lessons: 1. No one can get across on his own plank—it is broken. All your good deeds cannot avail. Many think they can get over on a good life, but all man's goodness is a broken plank.

2. No plank is stronger than its weakest point. This is true of your life. If it is weak in one point, it will break, and you will fall just as certainly as if it were weak in all points.

He that offends in one point, "is guilty of all."

3. You cannot get to the break to mend it. It is just behind you, and you will fall before you can reach it. There is no mending of past breaks with us.

4. We are not on *terra firma*, but over eternity; so don't let us feel too sure on our plank.

5. If you, or your friends, are on a broken plank, simply to remain where you are is certain doom. The bottomless pit is below. "He that believeth not is condemned already."

6. Don't think you can carry the least sin along with you, and yet get safely over. A bad thought will cause your ruin as certainly as a mountain of sin.

7. There is safety only in the palm of the hand stretched down from above. There, and nowhere else, is perfect security. Christ is God's only remedy for sin.

Are you in the palm of God's hand? or are you trusting to that poor old broken plank, **your own goodness?**

XIII.

Emblems of Time and Justice.

A wise man's heart discerneth both time and judgment. Ecc. 8:5.

[Objects.—A large funnel fitted with a cork in the small end. In this cork place a small glass funnel, and into this pour sand until it is full. A common sickle.]

The small funnel represents this life of each one of us. The large one represents the other life, or eternity. But the sizes of both are far out of proportion. If they were correct representations, the small one would be so small that it could hardly be seen, while the large one would extend out beyond this building, and on past the clouds, as far as the imagination could conceive of its reaching. Then that would more fittingly represent the other life, and the small one this life.

Or, take one of these grains of sand, and cut it into two pieces, and continue to do this till you could just see it; and then get a microscope that would magnify five thousand diameters, and cut the pieces in two, till you have the grain of sand divided into ten thousand parts. Hold one of these pieces on the point of a needle, and take it up in a balloon, and look at the earth, and think what is on the needle point, for you cannot see it, and then compare the two bodies in size. The minute one is time, and the earth is eternity. But a truer comparison would be to compare the little atom to the whole universe.

Go to the shore of the ocean, and stand upon the beach, and imagine that the great expanse before you goes on forever. That is eternity. Then stoop, and take up one little drop of water on your finger. This is time.

All time is almost nothing. How old are you? Twenty. If you were ninety, you would not be very old.

Here is a book that was printed two hundred and forty years ago, one hundred years before our Revolution, and only forty-eight years after Queen Elizabeth's time; and yet this is considered a very old book.

There are trees standing in California that John the Baptist might have preached under, if he had been in that American forest instead of in the wilderness of Judea. The Ptolemies of Egypt might have made their weapons of war from them if they had visited this land.

We may still look upon the remains of the Pharaoh of Egypt who ruled Israel with such an iron hand.

We may pick up shells, and handle the bones of animals that lived before the flood. Our common coal was growing in the forests thousands of years before that date. Yet that is not long ago. All time is but a little speck in space, a drop to the boundless ocean.

Then what must your life be? Even as a vapor.

I. Our little life is represented by the small funnel, which is filled with sand. So God fills each life with a definite amount of time.

1. The sand is no sooner poured in than it begins to run out, and it continues to do so without a break. So time begins to run out the moment we begin to live, and it never stops until our life is ended. Whether we are awake or asleep, or at business or pleasure, time keeps going. Every moment it is growing less. Like a ship in a great maelstrom, which goes nearer and nearer the centre and at last disappears, so the moments fly toward the point where the last one will disappear from view.

As the herds of buffalo used to be driven in between fences that continually narrowed together, and a fatal dart continued to pierce one and another, so we are going into the narrow quarters of time, and we too must fall one after another.

2. The sands fall so rapidly that one cannot count them. So time runs rapidly away, and many pay no heed to it, nor could we count its fleeting moments if we tried.

3. There is no calling these grains of sand back again. We cannot call time back again, if we would wish to do so. Baxter tells of a sick woman who called for time to come back again, but that was in vain.

4. The sands go into the invisible. We cannot see the future.

5. If you should watch the sand as it falls, you would see that it seems to go much faster when it has nearly all run out. In childhood the time does not go rapidly enough; the years seem too long. In old age the years seem to fly, till at last we count our life by hours and minutes.

II. When time is nearly gone with us, the sickle comes in as an emblem of the stern justice which cuts our life short.

1. This sickle seems to be an unmerciful thing. It is put around the standing grain, and mows all down in a most unmerciful way. So death is no respecter of persons. All have to go in their turn.

2. As the grain stands, apparently all unsuspecting what is to befall it, the sharp blade falls upon it, and suddenly down it goes. So time passes with us, and at a certain point death comes suddenly and cuts it off, and we fall.

No valuable moments of your life should be triflingly thrown away, for you cannot call them back. You should do your best every moment of time. Live so that, if you should be cut down any moment, you would be gathered with the wheat into the heavenly garner. A wise one's heart discerns the value of time, and his judgment leads him to be always ready for usefulness in life, and for glory in death.

XIV.

BREAD.

I am the bread of life. John 6: 35.

[OBJECTS.—Four small loaves of bread, baked hard, so that the bottoms can be cut out without destroying the shape of the loaves. One good large loaf.]

Bread is that on which one feeds. The text intimates that men spend money, labor, and time for, and live upon, that which is not true bread.

I. A decorated loaf, as an iced cake, only having candies on it to make it look as beautiful as possible. Before this is done, the bottom should be cut out carefully, and the inside of the loaf all taken out, leaving nothing but the crust. Put in a butterfly or some chaff. Replace the bottom and fasten it with pins. This is the finest looking loaf of all of them. It is the bread of pleasure. Any child would point to this loaf as his first choice, for it is the finest one we have. This is pleasant bread to look at; but get into it, and see what it really is. It proves to be vanity—a shell—good only to look at. This illustrates what the pleasures of the world are.

II. A loaf is brought out that has a dollar bill tied around it, or silver dollars pinned on it. A stone fills it. One cannot eat this, although the rich fool, mentioned in Luke 12, tried to do so, and many are trying still, and their soul can be no more satisfied than the foolish rich man. Don't forget that men with no money, are trying to feed on this bread, just as well as the richest men are. It is not the money, but the love of it, that does the harm.

III. Bread of anger, hatred, jealousy, or revenge. This has a small bottle of vinegar, some ashes, a scorpion, and anything of this nature inside. Cain fed on this, and many seem to delight to have no other kind. They love revenge—it is sweet to them—and they eat it often. They love the bread of deceit. Prov. 20: 17.

IV. The bread of death. On the bottom it has cross-bones and skull. Inside it has a wine glass, and a whiskey bottle, arsenic, and opium, or morphine. How many are feeding body and soul on these things! but they mean death to soul and body.

V. A good large loaf of bread. Break it, and it is sound and right. This loaf is good to eat. We are going to have this upon our table at the next meal. No death or vanity here, but food and health and life.

John 6:48: "I am the bread of life." Now preach on Jesus, the Bread of Life.

1. He alone is bread.
2. He is bread for the dead soul.
3. He meets every want.
4. But he must be eaten, not talked about, to be beneficial.
5. Not to feed on Him is a sure sign of death.
6. To partake of this Bread is to be forever blessed.

All this without money and without price.

XV.

THE LAMPS.

Then shall the kingdom of heaven be likened unto ten virgins, which took their lamps, and went forth to meet the bridegroom. And five of them were wise, and five were foolish. They that were foolish took their lamps, and took no oil with them: But the wise took oil in their vessels with their lamps. While the bridegroom tarried, they all slumbered and slept. And at midnight there was a cry made, Behold, the bridegroom cometh; go ye out to meet him. Then all those virgins arose, and trimmed their lamps. And the foolish said unto the wise, Give us of your oil; for our lamps are gone out. But the wise answered, saying, Not so; lest there be not enough for us and you: but go ye rather to them that sell, and buy for yourselves. And while they went to buy, the bridegroom came; and they that were ready went in with him to the marriage: and the door was shut. Afterward came also the other virgins, saying, Lord, Lord, open to us. But he answered and said, Verily I say unto you, I know you not. Watch therefore, for ye know neither the day nor the hour wherein the Son of man cometh. Matt. 25: 1 13.

[Objects are explained in the points below. Relate the story in a vivid manner, bringing it as a present event before the audience.]

The story is the picture of those who are expecting to be admitted into the Marriage Supper of the Lamb, some of whom are not making the necessary preparation. All those virgins intended to go in. If you had been there, you could not have told those who had oil and those who did not. Whatever difference there was in the looks and acts of those virgins, could be no guide to lead one to judge those who had oil and who had not. But when the bridegroom came, it was seen at once where the difference was. The oil in the lamp— the grace of God in the heart—is the one thing necessary.

I. Two fine lamps, one a piano lamp, and the other a beautiful table lamp. These represent a good class of persons, wealthy, educated, moral, refined, and capable of throwing out a great amount of light, and doing it beautifully. All these things are beautiful, and very useful, but they cannot take the place of the one thing needful—oil. If both have oil in, well; if not, then ill. Now let us light these two lamps, and see whether either one, or both, have oil in. Only one has; the other flickers and goes out. Picture to your mind two such persons being called for by the coming Bridegroom, and the consternation of the one having no oil, and the joy of the one who is ready.

II. These two tiny lamps represent two children. It is possible, and necessary, for children to be Christians. The Bridegroom also calls for many of them, and often suddenly, and He is soon to return, when all will need oil in their lamps. Some will have, and some will not have. Let us try these two tiny lamps, just as each boy and girl will be tried. One lights, and the other does not. Set the little lantern that has the oil in down at the foot of the oilless piano lamp, and see the contrast. A child Christian has something that a great governor has not, who is not a Christian. Oil is a necessity to the child, as well as to the grown person. Which one of these two little lamps are you, my boy? Which one are you, my girl?

III. Here are two small tin lamps painted red, having reflectors on. Part of the chimneys are also painted red. These are two persons who have made a profession of their faith in Christ, at some time. They have both professed to have been washed in the blood of Christ from their sins, and have the power to reflect Christ, and when their light shines, to show no other light but the blood of Christ. Both have had oil put into them, both have thus received grace. Try them with the light. One burns, and the other does not. One has oil, and the other has not. The oil has leaked out of some tiny hole, which cannot be seen in the latter one. The wick is short and was not saturated with oil, and so it will not burn at all. Here is the danger: some small hole may be in the professed Christian's lamp, from which is flowing the precious oil, all unknown and unsuspected, and when, at the coming of the Bridegroom, the vessel is looked into, it is found, when alas! too late, that there is no oil. The small hole in the Christian's lamp is his greatest danger. Here is a larger and more pretentious lamp than the small one from which the oil leaked, but no one would be deceived with this one, it has so large a hole in it. (The lamp has a very large hole broken into it.) No one would think of putting oil into this one, till it was properly repaired. But it is far different with the other lamp. I did not once suspect that it would leak, when I put the oil into it. No hole at all can be seen in it. The large hole in the large lamp represents an infidelity or scepticism, which does not believe in God, the Bible, or any hereafter. No one would think of such a thing as the grace of God being in such a heart. A radical change is seen to be needed before that one can indulge any hope of salvation. But with the other, it is far different, as no hole is seen. Suppose there is a small drop of oil seen at the bottom of the lamp once in a while; that is not enough to frighten a sensible person; it might a weak and narrow-minded one. So the oil slips away till the awful day of trial comes and then the true state is seen when too late. 1. Doubts that are tolerated are one little hole—doubting God and his Word. 2. Dabbling in worldliness is another little hole, which seems to be of no account. But he who will be a friend of the world, will surely be the enemy of God. 3. Ease in Zion, indifference to the needs of a lost world. Not bearing the cross for Christ. 4. Another is a loose conscience about little sins—white lies for policy's sake—taking a little advantage in dealing when you have a chance; neglecting a careful obedience to

God's law, such as the Sabbath, etc.; in short, going as near to the line between sin and obedience as possible, and yet hoping to keep God's grace. 5. Letting malice grow in the heart, which is sure to crowd out grace, is another. All these are little holes and, if not watched, will ruin the soul's prospects of going in to the marriage feast of Christ.

IV. The poor, broken, and smoky lamps are those people who do not have many of this world's goods, and do have an abundance of its troubles, and often much poverty. Surely such people ought to have oil in their vessels, for if they have few comforts here, they certainly ought to be sure of them hereafter. But trying them proves that only one has the oil. Poverty does not prove that the one has the riches of grace, sorrows do not make the joys of Christ in the heart, clouds cannot make God's sunshine in the soul. People are often led to think so, but none of these things can take the place of Christ in the heart. Many such will be surprised, as well as many rich people, when the Bridegroom comes.

V. These bull's-eye lanterns are those people who are thoughtful, careful, and watchful. They are those in the world who are wise, and look out well for the future. They also guard well the interests of those around them, such as their children and friends. Such shall also be summoned before the Master, and have to pass the test. We try these two, and see one of them to be wanting in the one thing needful. How people watch the approach of sickness in their homes! how they watch for temporal advancement! how careful for pleasure, the good opinion of others, and for everything in this life! but, oh, how they sleep while the Bridegroom is tarrying a little! How careless about eternity! If this one thing is not found in your vessel when at some unexpected moment in the near future you are called, then you are undone forever! No going to buy then; it will be too late.

The door will be shut, and shut never to be opened! But now it is open, and you may obtain the one thing needful—Christ in your soul. Will you have Him?

XVI.

Testing by Fire.

But who may abide the day of his coming? and who shall stand when he appeareth? for he is like a refiner's fire, and like fullers' soap: And he shall sit as a refiner and purifier of silver. Mal. 3: 2, 3.

[Asbestos rope, from one who works around an engine; asbestos paper, from a wholesale drug store (Eimer & Amen, Eighteenth Street and Third Avenue, N. Y.), ten cents' worth; some alcohol, a Bunsen burner, or any lamp, flax, stubble, hemp, cord like the asbestos cord, and paper like the asbestos paper.]

I. Burn a small piece of paper, and some rope, saturated in alcohol. What the fire is to the paper, and rope, that God is to a sinner saturated in his sins; so says the text, and also Mal. 4: 1 and Heb. 12: 29. There is this difference, viz., these seem to be annihilated (but in reality they are not, having only changed their form), which is not the case with one who is consumed in his sins by the divine flame.

Isa. 33:14: "Who among us shall dwell with everlasting burnings?" Also Matt. 25:46. This rope and this paper burned in the fire, only because they were inflammable material, and in a hot fire.

II. Here is a material which cannot be burned. Its very name signifies "unconsumable": asbestos, a kind of rock, or mineral. Now try to burn the asbestos rope and paper, saturated in alcohol. The alcohol burns off, but the rope, heavy paper, and even the lightest paper are not at all affected by the fire. Now, there is another kind of rock which also is not affected by the fire, and that Rock is the One on which the true church of God is being built. Every sinner who builds on this Rock is secure against every fire, for he becomes himself a part of that Rock. This is the part of the sinner which cannot sin; it is the "seed" of God which remains in him (1 John 3:9), and it is the part which "cannot die" (John 11:26). Also Ex. 3:2. When any one with this Rock nature in him, comes to the smelter's fire, he is right in his element; the fire can only do good, and not harm.

III. Burn leaves of paper and asbestos which look alike. These should be saturated in alcohol, and bound together with wire. This represents the trial of a church in the Judgment. Persons may look alike, be in the same church or family, and yet be of very different natures, like these two kinds of paper. But the day of fire will show the difference. Some will be found to be wheat, and will be gathered; and others will be found to be chaff, and will be burned with unquenchable fire (Matt. 3:12).

IV. Asbestos rope braided in with some of the common kind, and asbestos paper with thread sewed through it; these are saturated with alcohol, and burned. These represent the true Christian who has sin still in him, which must be burned out of him in the Refiner's fire. The fire looks as if it were burning all up; but never fear, it can only burn the cotton out—it cannot hurt the Rock nature. Mal. 3:3. Don't be afraid of the "fiery trial" (1 Pet. 4:12). If you are a Christian, and are in the fire, it may be because God has given you a nature which He sees is worth refining you for; which He wants to develop in you.

V. (Hold a piece of asbestos paper in a candle, and get soot on it, and then hold in the hot flame.) Asbestos paper blackened with the smoke and soot, is cleansed when held in the hot flame; the paper itself is made whiter by the flame. Just so it is with the Christian. The fiery trials first burn out the cotton, and then if he is held in the flame a little longer, he becomes white and beautiful. For a Christian to suffer, is God's vote of confidence in him. He could have trusted but few of His children to be put in the hot flame that He permitted Job to be put into. It is said that Charlemagne had an asbestos tablecloth, which he used to throw into the fire after dinner, for the astonishment of his guests. He knew that the fire could not harm it; it only purified it. If a child of God is in the fire, it is by no means because the Father has lost interest in His child.

Conclusion: Man's only hope is in the new and divine nature. Our natural man, self, will burn in the presence of God like this flax in the flame (Isa. 1:31) or as this stubble in this flame (Mal. 4:1). (Hold the flax or stubble in the flame, being careful not to become burned by the sudden flame on the flax.)

Jesus Christ is the only one Who can take the burn all out of fire (Dan. 3). Fire could not burn Shadrach, Meshach, and Abednego when Jesus—"the form of the fourth like the Son of God"—was with them. All your afflictions cannot burn you; upon your body the fire will have no power, nor will a hair of your head be singed, neither will your coat be changed, nor the smell of fire pass on you, if you have Christ with you. Only the one who has Jesus walk with him in the fires of sickness, sorrows, bereavements, losses, and disappointments can walk and not be burned; and the closer to Jesus he walks, the less smell of fire there will be on him. Some parade their troubles, they smell much of fire, but they are not the ones who walk close to Jesus when in the furnace. Mark that, for it never fails. If you know none of these fires now, you will know them, for they will soon be burning upon you; they are all around you even now. Then you will feel the need of the Rock nature in you, and around you.

But if you will need Jesus with you in the furnaces of this life, how much more you will in the "great day of his wrath." Who can stand when the One appeareth who is Himself like the smelter's fire? Woe to Shadrach, Meshach, and Abednego if they get into the furnace with no form of the fourth with them! Woe to you if you are found in the Judgment without the robe on you which protects from that fire—Jesus' righteousness!

But blessed is the one who has Jesus in his heart; blessed is the one who has the sin burned out of him here. The gold that has passed through the smelter's fire here, will have nothing left that will burn over there. He shall skip and gambol as calves let out of the stall (Mal. 4: 2). All the fires will be past, and nothing but "green fields beyond the swelling flood." But you must have this preparation here. Take *on* Jesus, receive Him *into* your heart. *He* is *eternal life*, and the fires of sin, afflictions, death, and the Judgment cannot touch that life.

XVII.

Corn.

Herein is my Father glorified, that ye bear much fruit. John 15:8.

[OBJECTS.—Two large ears of corn; one ear of sweet-corn; one of pop-corn; one broken ear; one ear with corn nearly off, exposing the cob; one long cob with corn all gone; one black, smutty ear; one on which no corn ever developed, and two in which merely the cobs have formed.]

These ears of corn represent different degrees of fruit-bearing in men and women.

I. Here are two good ears. One is red and the other is yellow. One has black spots on it. These represent good, whole-hearted Christians, who are different in Christian work and natural make-up, yet both are valuable. They are slightly imperfect at best. These ears are long, indicating much ability for fruit-bearing, and which shows well to the world.

II. The short, rough-looking ear is not so attractive to look at, nor does it make so big a show. Yet it is just as valuable. It is delicious *sweet-corn*. This is a Christian whose work and life are sweet, because there is much love in both. He is not so pretentious as some; but what he lacks in that, he makes up in loveliness of nature. The ear is not so long as the others, but there is corn on the cob to the very end. If you have not so great ability as some, you can be as valuable by being sweet in your life. You can be full of love.

III. Here is a small, black ear which is not so attractive as either of the others, but it is full of corn. It is pop-corn. The worst side of this one is its outside. Many Christians appear worse in their outward life than they are within. They have a way of showing all the black in them. They may be daring, outspoken, faithful Christians, who are not so sweet as others, but really just as valuable to the Master. They are out and out for Christ, and the right, and make no compromises with the world in any way. So they are not so highly appreciated usually; but to see their real beauty one must wait till they are in the popper of severe affliction or trials, and then they seem to blow out white and beautiful. Some of the strongest and most beautiful Christians were of the pop-corn nature. Luther was one, while Melancthon was of the sweet-corn kind.

IV. Here is an ear that is broken in two. It had much fruit once, but has lost half it had. I suspect it got under the *hoof* in some manner. What fruit it has is good, but it has only half of what it ought to have. This is a Christian whose lifework and usefulness are cut short by some calamity, misfortune, or sin, which is more frequently the case. He gets perhaps for *once* where he ought not to be, or he yields to some sudden temptation, and it cuts off his usefulness for the future, and largely destroys the good he did in other days. It often is the case of a Christian who becomes unequally yoked together with an unbeliever for life, in marriage. Beware! for this is a more frequent source of permanent injury in the lifework of Christians than many are aware!

V. Here is a long cob, with but little fruit. Here are large powers once developed, but now almost entirely lying waste. Squirrels and mice have gnawed off the fruit. This is a believer in whom the cares of the world and the deceitfulness of riches have eaten off the fruit.

VI. Here is a long cob, but no corn. Here were grand powers, but they are gone now. This one has been despoiled of all his fruit, and ability. Drink, bad thoughts, bad reading, neglect of duty, have resulted in the ruin of the fruit of the life, and destroyed the power for any further usefulness. This one is like the branch not bearing fruit—it is only fit to be cast aside. The saddest sight possible, is to look upon one who was once a hopeful and useful Christian, whose whole life and influence are like this corn-cob—barren of any good fruit.

VII. The next two ears are worthless ones. One is covered with smut, so that any little fruit it has is ruined. The other is dwarfed, and the corn never could grow. The reason for this is the bad soil in which it grew. It was a cold, damp soil, and hence these ears. Bad company is the difficulty. One who gets in with vile associates will grow vile, black sins. He may try to be a Christian, and bring forth some fruit for Christ, but it is invariably like that on this smutty ear, or like that on the dwarfed ear. It is doubtful if such corn as this will ever be garnered. If it is ever saved, it will be as by fire.

VIII. The next, are two worthless ears in every respect. The most that can be said for them is that they look a little like corn, but they are not. They only have the form. There is neither corn nor cob; and since there is nothing but the empty husks, they are fit only to be cast out and trodden under foot. The Master, at the harvest-time, will not hesitate a moment about saving these. But they have all the reward that any will ever have, who aim only at the form of Christian life, and care not for its life and power.

Learn some lessons from this corn: 1. In order to bear fruit, you must be planted, and *die*. Self and sin must be killed.

2. You must be in the right soil—in Christ.

3. You must have dew and rain—the Holy Spirit and His grace.

4. There must be heat, love. Corn *cannot* grow without *heat*. A lack of this is largely the cause of all the bad ears we see. Love will bear fruit *every time*.

5. For a good growth, there must be sunlight. The light of the Word must be diligently sought.

6. Wind and storms are important too, as they fasten the roots and stretch them out, and blow off pollen on to the silk. These things are a necessity. If you are a Christian, and are having storms, you may rest assured that they are not sent for your ruin, but rather that you may have increased usefulness. You are doing a service you never could do without them.

XVIII.

CRADLES.

When I was a child, I spake as a child, I understood as a child, I thought as a child: but when I became a man, I put away childish things. 1 Cor. 13: 11.

[OBJECTS. — Two cradles — one an ordinary babe's cradle, and a doll's cradle.]

A babe's cradle is used to rock the child, so as to satisfy it when it is cross. It is also used to rock the child when it is tired, so as to give it rest, and give the parents peace. Rocking the cradle also puts the child asleep.

The doll's cradle is used to rock a make-believe baby, one which has no life. There are some who are called Christians who are not even babies, though they may look like them. They have no life, yet they very often have to have their little cradles, to look as much as possible like a real live baby. But one can usually tell whether it is a doll or a live baby, if he is around them very long.

In their Christian life, some men and women are children, and some children are men and women. Paul, in 1 Cor. 3:1, says: "And I, brethren, could not speak unto you as unto spiritual, but as unto carnal, even as unto babes in Christ." This, and also the text, show that some men and women are babes. There are some things which show whether one is a babe, or a man or woman.

I. What he eats tells. If he eats milk and not meat, he is a babe (1 Cor. 3:2). Who ever saw a babe eating beefsteak? He would starve on it. He has no teeth, and besides it is too strong for his stomach. Some Christians never get beyond the doctrines of sin and forgiveness. They cannot take in, nor have they any interest in, the doctrine of the enduement of the Holy Spirit for sanctification and service. They have to be rocked in the cradle of first experiences all their lives.

II. A baby is one who cannot help himself, or others. He has always to be helped, and expects nothing else. Babies are very nice, but would not be so nice if they remained babies all the time, till they became fifty years old. Babies usually grow, and get out of the cradle, and then rock their little brothers and sisters, till they too get out of the cradle. Some Christians seem never to get above the point of always needing help, and are never able to help others.

III. Little children often get cross very easily, and it takes the whole family to coax them into good humor. They require a great deal of petting to make it agreeable to live with them, and this uses up a great deal of fathers' and mothers' valuable time.

Every church ought to have a large cradle, not to put the babies in, who come to church with their parents, for they seldom ever come nowadays, but to put the spiritual babes in, who need petting and coaxing. If they have their way, they would have the minister spend all his time about the cradle rocking them, and the larger brothers and sisters would be about with rattles and gymnastic games to entertain.

It would be a blessing if such cradles could be run by water or electric motors. It is not at all an enviable position to be in such a cradle, for the time is sure to come when the bough will bend, the cradle will fall, and down will come rock-a-by-baby and all.

IV. A little babe is always easily led astray. It does not always know the right path, and can be easily directed into a wrong one. There are many spiritual children who are "tossed to and fro, and carried about with every wind of doctrine, by the sleight of men, and cunning craftiness, whereby they lie in wait to deceive" (Eph. 4: 14). They are easily thrown off their balance by every new teacher, or are led easily into error or sin. It is a great thing for them to fall in with a new teacher who has strange mysteries to reveal, which few have ever thought of. The reason for this little stability, is because they are babes in understanding (I. Cor. 14: 20).

V. Paul says, in I. Cor. 3: 3, that envying, strife, and divisions are a sign of the childhood state. It is very often that little children show their envy in the use of their playthings.

The playthings of this world are often the cause of great discord, and envy, among those who are called God's children.

The way to get out of the cradle is to *grow*. The one who *breathes, eats,* and *works* will *grow*, and become a man. Pray, study the Bible, and work for Christ and others, and you will *grow*, and you will surely be out of the cradle, for you will become a man and you will put away childish things.

XIX.

The Spider and the Fly.

That they may recover themselves out of the snare of the devil, who are taken captive by him at his will. II. Tim. 2: 26.

[OBJECT.—A spider and web, with a fly caught in it, if possible. If they cannot be obtained, a web made of wire and threads, like the cut, will answer.]

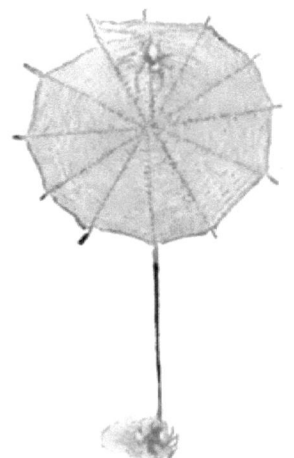

I. The spider is the deadly enemy of the fly. He sets his net in its path, and does all he can to catch the poor fly. So we are taught in the text, and in other places in the Bible, that the Devil is our deadly enemy. Every one who comes into the world has conflict with him. The scorpion and spider are much alike; they are of the same family. In the Scripture Satan is likened to the scorpion. He has power to do men great harm. He always sits in our *path*. Some of his nets placed in the path are the hope of worldly gain, pleasures of the world, doubts against the Scriptures, lusts, and putting off one's salvation.

II. Give the spider a foothold, and he is so skilful that he can put in his net. Give Satan a little chance at you, by harboring evil desires, and he will put in a net to catch you.

III. The spider's web is spun from his own bowels. More than six hundred separate strands go to make the one slender thread which we see stretching out from her body. Satan's webs are all woven from his own imagination. He makes one believe that his offers are very valuable, but he has a cable of more than six hundred strands to throw around his victim at the first opportunity.

IV. The spider can run over her web very deftly. No other insect can do it. Satan seems to be able to run over his webs so easily, that they hardly seem more than playthings. Temptation, before yielded to, seems a thing that can be easily and safely toyed with, but after yielding to it, you seem to be entangled in a thousand meshes.

V. As the spider goes over the net, she deposits a gummy substance at the cross-sections, which causes the web to cling to its victim, when once it touches him. Notice how Satan's nets cling to one, when the smallest threads are thrown around the soul. The smallest sins fasten themselves to the one committing them;

and how difficult they are to be shaken off! Try to shake off any bad habit and see.

VI. There are several kinds of spiders—the common garden and house spider, the trapdoor spider, the wolf spider, the leaping and water spiders. These all have their own peculiar way of catching their victims. This is like Satan, who transforms himself in any way that will best catch our souls. At one time he comes as an angel of light, and we think it some good spirit prompting us. Then he may come as a lion, to frighten and discourage us in our Christian life.

VII. After the spider has put up her web, she then goes and conceals herself, and waits for the fly. So Satan is very careful to conceal himself in all his plans to catch us. He tries to make us believe that all his temptations are our thoughts.

VIII. The spider lives all along the line of the web, and the least little touch of any part of it she feels instantly. Satan knows very well when one comes near to him, or his nets. He lives amid all his snares.

IX. Notice how the spider deals with her prey. A good-sized fly comes buzzing along, and, running its body against the web, gives it a shake. Instantly

> "The spider's touch, how exquisitely fine,
> Feels at each thread and lives along the line,"

"and almost before you can see her, she has darted from her hiding-place to the centre of the web. Here she herself gives it a shake to find whether it will be answered, showing that a live object is causing the disturbance. The unfortunate fly quivers in the toils, betraying its whereabouts, and straight the spider darts upon it, and with one sharp bite ends its life. It is not, however, strictly speaking, with her mouth that she has bitten it, but with two poison fangs which hang down over the mouth." When she seized her prey, these were opened, and the sharp points, driven into the fly's body, gave out poison from their tips, and quickly put an end to its life.

While she is busy eating this meal, an interruption occurs. "A fresh shake of the web informs her that a new victim is caught, and she hastens to the spot. This time it is a strong night beetle which is caught in the toils, and she cannot grapple with him so rashly as with the fly, while his struggles threaten to break the net. In this dilemma she has a stratagem ready. Pressing her spinnerets against the web, she begins to weave around him a covering of silk, and, going closer and closer as his legs are entangled, she twists him round and round with her feet till, quite enveloped, he can struggle no longer and receives his death-blow.

"But if by chance it had been a wasp, and she dreaded its sting, she herself would have torn the strands of the web, and let it fly away sooner than run the risk of being the conquered instead of the conqueror."

All this has its lessons for every one who is dallying with temptation. Satan knows when to strike the blow that fills the soul with his deadly poison. He does not do it till he has sufficiently wound up his victim in the net.

We are no more safe from his nets, than the fly is from the web. But if we call for aid at once, we have a Friend who can deliver us out of his snares. Beware lest you be taken captive by him at his will: take the sword of the Spirit, and his nets will fall before it.

XX.

Wonders of the Sun.

The Lord God is a sun. Ps. 84: 11.

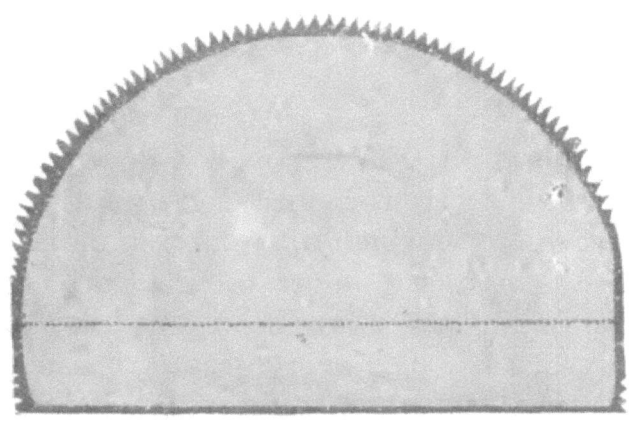

OBJECT.—On a large paper draw a circle fifty-five inches in diameter. This represents the sun. Make the outline heavy, with a red-lead pencil, say an inch thick. Inside of this circle, and using the same centre, draw another circle, thirty inches in diameter. This represents the orbit of the moon. At the centre of the circles, make a round spot one-half inch in diameter, having a red centre. This is the earth. Draw one hundred and eleven of these in a straight line across the large circle.

These represent the number of globes, the size of the earth, which would be needed to reach across the sun. All this is to show the comparative sizes of the sun and the earth.]

In the text, the Jehovah God, or Jesus, likens Himself to the sun. Let us notice some of the things in which the sun resembles Christ.

The sun is the most familiar orb in the heavens, and yet it is almost the least known about, because of its very great brilliancy. It cannot be looked at except through smoked glass, or when it is hidden behind the moon, as a sort of a veil from its glory. The brilliancy of the sun hinders one from seeing what it is composed of; just as one sees a piece of glass lying on the earth, which is reflecting the sunlight, and is so bright that he can see only the bright surface, and cannot tell of what the object is composed.

There is no name in this world so familiar as the name of Christ, and yet there is a world of mystery about Him. Man fails as much in comprehending Him now, as he failed centuries ago. Like the sun, He is a mystery, and all the ages of eternity will not fully unfold His nature, for He is infinite. The very brilliancy of His character is that which blinds the eye, and He can be looked at only through the veil of His human nature, as Israel looked at Moses' fading glory.

I. Consider the sun in its relation to the earth and the other planets.

1. The sun is the centre of the solar system, and holds them all steady in their courses, as they revolve around him.

So Christ is the centre of all life, and He holds them all steady as they move on, but ever about Him. There is no life, or power that is not from Him. "In Him we live, and move, and have our being." Not a breath is drawn that He is not the giver of; not a hand is raised, that He does not give the strength. He is the centre of all life and motion, whether of men, animals, or of the universe. He holds the sun, that holds the planets in their courses.

2. Consider the comparative sizes of the sun and the earth, as represented on this chart. The large circle represents the sun, and the very small black dot the earth. It takes one hundred and eleven of the small dots, in a line, to reach across the space which represents the sun. The sun would make more than 1,380,000 globes equal in size to the earth, if divided and moulded. The moon is 240,000 miles from the earth; it, and the earth, could both be put into the sun, if it were hollow, and the moon could continue to revolve around the earth, as it does now, and at the same distance, and yet be over

200,000 miles from the shell of the sun. It is more than 500 times larger than all the planets and satellites put together.

Its distance from the earth is 92,000,000 miles. One would have to travel around the earth 3,800 times in order to travel as great a distance as it is to the sun. Or, if one had started on a journey to the sun, in the year 1492, when Columbus discovered America, and had travelled at the rate of 500 miles a day, he would have to travel over one hundred years yet before he would reach the sun.

The vastness of the sun, and its great distance from the earth, well illustrate the superiority of Christ to man and all created beings combined. Only this comparison falls infinitely short of showing how much superior He is to all human creatures. A million creatures, as great as man, might be created hourly for a million years, and all combine their greatness, and they would fall infinitely short of equalling the one Christ; for He is the one self-existent being of the universe; the divine One, surpassing all our conception of His greatness and vast removal from man, while He, at the same time, comes like the sun's rays, and touches each one. He is never too far away to flood the world with His light and power, which He is doing momentarily. The sun's rays fall upon the earth, and promote the growth of all living things, and so are treasured up in all animal bodies as heat, and in the fibre of every vegetable or tree, finally to be brought out again as heat or motion. So every fire burns, every train moves, and every animal moves, because the sun has poured in his heat, to furnish the fuel to do it with.

How true this is of Christ in the spiritual world. Every holy thought, every loving work, every pitying look, every feeling of sympathy, or every good deed is only the light reflected from Him. The light shines from the "Sun of righteousness" upon the souls of men, and is treasured up by them as latent heat, to be called out when the occasion offers. No one can live in this world, because of the death of Christ, and not be benefited by His rays of light.

3. The earth is constantly depending upon the sun for its heat, and holding power, but the sun is not so depending upon the earth. Christ is not dependent upon any person for either His glory or happiness. But the extent that we are dependent upon Him will never be known. The desolation and darkness, which we can conceive that the world would now be in, had there never been any sun, is only a faint picture of what our condition would be, had Christ never lived.

4. The earth has a centrifugal impulse,

which it probably originally received from the sun, and which tends to drive it out into space. There is at the same time a centrifugal force, or gravitation, exerted by the sun to draw the earth back into its bosom. These two forces hold the earth in its proper position. Some men say that the time will come when the earth will fall into the bosom of the sun, of which it was originally a part. These are like the forces that God has exerted over man. Originally He created man in His own likeness, breathed in his nostrils His own Spirit, and sent man out into the world. This was the centrifugal force. Since the fall, He has been putting forth His mighty pulling power, to keep man in his proper course, until at last he shall be cleansed and received into the Father's bosom again.

If gravitation of the sun were suspended, in order to retain the earth in its present orbit it would require a cable that could sustain over a quintillion of tons weight, or a hundred million times a billion tons—a weight and strength transcending all human comprehension.

How like the drawing power of Christ! "I, if I be lifted up, will draw all men unto me." And this drawing power of Christ is his love. Dr. Newton tells of a Mr. and Mrs. Stone who had an orphan nephew, by the name of Jack, who was utterly bad, and who had to be confined in a room and fed upon prisoners' fare, to punish him for cruelly treating his cousin Susie. She pitied him, and took his place, and ate his bread and water, that he might go out and enjoy the beautiful day. Her love proved to be such a drawing power to Jack that it broke him completely.

This is something like the drawing power of the love of Jesus. There is no sin that it will not draw one out of, if it has any chance at all.

II. Consider the sun by itself.

1. Little is known of the constituent parts of the sun. The spectroscope reveals the presence of many of the elements on the earth. The sun has two atmospheres; one non-luminous, and the other luminous, which is composed of living waves of fire. These flames sometimes shoot out 400,000 miles, and with incredible velocity.

The two atmospheres are like the two natures in Christ; the divine is the luminous and striking one, while his human nature is the non-luminous atmosphere.

The halo thrown out from His holy life on earth, sprang from His luminous or divine atmosphere. This is the atmosphere of His life, which has led one to exclaim: "Rationalism cannot look at Him closely to-day except on its knees."

2. The sun's heat is very powerful, and far reaching. It has power to make alive, and to kill. In the spring it vivifies the grass, and later on it kills by the stroke of its heat.

So Christ quickens the dead soul, and is also a consuming fire to all who persist in sin.

3. The sun has healing for the sick in his rays. This is a common fact of experience.

So the Sun of Righteousness arises with healing in His wings, or rays, for every malady of the soul. Every distress in life, is relieved by the cheering and healing presence of Christ.

4. Like the sun, He shines for all. A million eyes can look up to, and a million sick bodies can be bathed in the sun's rays at the same instant. Millions can call upon Christ at once, and all receive His presence and power. He is no respecter of persons.

5. The more we study the nature of a sunbeam, the more we admire its beauty, and the mystic powers of its prismatic colors. Nothing can be exposed to it without undergoing a change.

So the more we know of Christ, the more we love and admire the beauties of His character, and wonder at the mystery of His power over us and others. No one can come near Him, and not be changed.

6. The sunlight may fall on all manner of

corruption and foulness, and yet remain free from contamination.

So Jesus visits the vilest hearts, and shines away the corruption, and remains, as when He was upon earth, pure from every stain of sin. He, nor those who shine by light borrowed from Him, are never corrupted in their work of shining away the sink-holes of sin.

The sunlight changes all, but is itself never changed.

7. While his rays are life-giving and cleansing, at the same time they are wonderfully powerful in driving death on into a state of corruption. Dead creatures cannot long be left exposed to his power.

Christ's power is wonderfully drawing and life-giving; but the dead soul that resists Him, it drives swiftly into awful corruption. Watch the corruption of any soul who continues to resist the calls of the Spirit. How swiftly he goes down!

III. Consider some of the results of abusing the benefits he brings.

1. To receive benefit from the rays of the sun, we must remain in the atmosphere of the earth. Here the rays are refracted, and softened, and are most beneficial. If one could ascend in a balloon above the atmosphere, all there would be utter blackness, and the sun's rays would pierce him through on one side,

while he would be chilled to death on the other side.

For one to flee out of the atmosphere in which Christ shines, is to run into darkness and death. And there are many such atmospheres abroad, that look inviting for souls to flee into. Beware of them.

2. One may deliberately put out his eyes, while the sun is shining, which will leave him as much in the darkness as if the sun were blotted from the heavens.

Many, by their wilful sins, deliberately put out the eyesight of their souls. It is not that Jesus ceases to be loving, that men are lost, but that they destroy the last remnant of the light that would lead them to Him. This is why they are irreparably lost.

Lessons: 1. Pull down the shades of evil desire, and resistance to God, and let the glorious sunlight into your soul.

2. Those who walk in His light, know where they are going. What their end will be, is a matter of certainty to them.

3. There is no night in the land to which they go. Will you go there too?

XXI.

Light and Darkness in the Heart.

For ye were sometimes darkness, but now are ye light in the Lord: walk as children of light. Eph. 5: 8.

[Objects.—Two clear glasses, one of which  has a heart painted on it in red paint. Put black water into one, and oil into the other, both being full. An ordinary postal card, or a piece of thin tin, and a plate to set the glasses on.]

I. The first part of the text says that the Ephesians were sometimes darkness, and I suppose they were no more darkness than any one else. Every one is by nature a child of darkness; that is, the soul of each one of us is dark, just as this water in the glass, having the heart on it, is black. By nature, our soul is dark, and all our deeds are also dark, in the sight of God. To Him, our nature is so black that he calls us darkness. Look at this glass of black water, and see just how you look to God, if you are not a Christain.

II. This glass of pure oil represents the Spirit of Christ. Oil is often used in the Scriptures as a symbol, or type, of the Holy Spirit. This Oil, God desires to put into every dark soul. But the soul is already full of its own blackness, just as this glass is now full of black water; and the heart is covered, just as the glass is now covered with this piece of tin. The way the Spirit of Christ gets into our dark heart, is just the way the oil gets into the glass now having the black water in it. (Put your fingers on the piece of tin covering the glass of black water, and hold it firmly down to the glass and invert the glass over the glass of oil. Then holding on to the glasses with the fingers, move the tin which is between them with the thumbs, so that there is a small opening, and the black water, and the oil, will gradually change glasses.)

1. You noticed that the black glass was first inverted. This is the way our sinful lives are first changed. There is a complete turning of the life about, often a turning and overturning of the whole life. Our ideas, thoughts, acts, and plans are turned, when the Holy Spirit comes near the heart.

2. Then there was an opening made, so that the two liquids could change places. So the

heart must be opened to receive the Spirit of Christ. The door of the heart must be opened, which is being fully willing to receive Christ within, as Saviour, Master, and Friend (Rev. 3:20).

3. Notice that the blackness of the one glass was driven out, by making an opening, and letting the oil in. Bad thoughts, doubts, lying, stealing, and other things in our lives that are black, are not going to be driven out by our merely trying very hard to drive them out. What we are to do, is to open our heart, and pray God to send the Holy Spirit into it, and He will come in, and out will go the blackness without fail. We are bound to have our hearts filled with something. If it is self, or sin, then it cannot be Christ. But if we want the sin out, we must open the door, and keep it open, to let Him come in. It is either Christ in, and sin out, or it is sin in, and Christ out; for the two cannot occupy the same heart at the same time. "Ye cannot serve God and mammon."

III. The glass that had the black water in it, now has the light oil in it. This represents the change in the heart of every one who becomes a Christian. "For ye were sometimes darkness, but now are ye light in the Lord." But to become a Christian is not all there is to be done. The other part of the text must also be heeded, " walk as children of light." Now you are to watch against the same evil, that was once driven out of the heart. The blackness is without, but it is all about you, seeking an opportunity to get in again. (Cover the glass with the black liquid in it, and invert it over the glass of oil as before. Make a small opening, and in comes the black liquid to the glass with the heart painted on it. It slowly fills the whole glass and drives out the oil.)

1. When the glass of black water was resting inverted over the glass of oil, it represented the close contact of evil to every Christian heart, only waiting to get in. Satan is continually about the heart, only waiting for the first opportunity to thrust in the blackness of sin.

2. At first a little hole is made. It may be a lack of secret prayer, or some evil thought, or lack of love, and then come the doubts, and bad company, a refusal to bear crosses, and the like, and soon the heart is full of blackness again. Then it is discovered that the heart is backslidden, which is simply giving a place to the Devil to lodge in the heart; and where he is, the Spirit of God cannot dwell.

If the piece of tin between these two glasses is removed, and the glasses are shaken, still the oil will not mix with the black water. (If you do this, the glasses must have smooth edges and be held firmly together.) You cannot mix the Spirit of Christ and Satan. They cannot be made to mix in the heart, or in society. Many seem to think that they will, at least a little, but it only results in driving out the Holy Spirit, and letting Satan's darkness take His place.

Another thing to notice, is that this exchange is not made all at once. The darkness, if allowed a little hole, will come in little by little, till all the light is crowded out. So the least opening to sin must be guarded against. Our hearts do not backslide from God all at once.

The time will soon come when God will show what each has in his heart. Open your heart to Christ, and then watch carefully, and pray against small holes through which sin can enter; "For ye were sometimes darkness, but now are ye light in the LORD: walk as children of light."

XXII.

THE VISIBLE AND INVISIBLE WRITING.

For God shall bring every work into judgment, with every secret thing, whether it be good, or whether it be evil. Eccl. 12:14.

And the fire shall try every man's work of what sort it is. I. Cor. 3:13.

[OBJECTS.—Take a piece of starch as large as a pea, and dissolve it in about three tablepoonfuls of water, and then boil it till it is clear. Add as much water again, and then put in three or four drops of tincture of iodine, and all turns a dark blue. Take some sulphuric acid, and add seven times its quantity in water, to make it dilute. Write, with a gold or quill pen in large letters, any message you like, on a large clean sheet of white paper. Let it dry, and no writing can be seen. This represents the inner life of a person. Write on the same paper, with a stick or small brush, anything you wish with the blue ink. If the writing of both is printed letters, it can be seen all the better. This latter writing is to represent the outer life of a person, what he seems. What one seems may be very different from what he is inside. Two or three sheets of paper, for as many classes of persons as you wish to represent, may be written upon.

These two sheets of paper I hold in my hands, you see, have very different reading upon them. The one in my right hand reads: "A Large Giver, Very Religious, A Grand Fellow, Saved." The one in my left hand reads: "An Enemy of Happiness, Narrow, False, A Crank, No Christian." These two sheets of paper represent two classes of persons in the world. The large writing you see on them is what people think of them. This is their outward life. But each one has also an inward life, which may be like the outward life, but usually is not just like the outward one, and often is just the opposite of what the world reads it to be.

I will hold the one in my right hand over the flame of the lamp, and see what the fire will reveal. (When it is well heated, the writing in acid will appear black, and the writing in iodine and starch disappears—the invisible appears, while the visible disappears.) The fire has brought out the real character of the hidden writing, and has swept away that which was so prominent before. The reading now is: "Deceived, False, Lost, Loves the Praise of Men More than the Praise of God."

I hold the one that was in my left hand in the flame, and see the result. Here again the prominent writing of public opinion vanishes, and that which could not be seen before now appears in prominent letters. This too is a great change; for instead of terms of contempt, they are: "Faithful, Uncompromising, True to God and Man, Saved." Here is a third sheet of paper, with this writing on it: "A Sincere Christian, Out and Out for God, Kind, Has Enemies, Is Forgiving." We will hold this too in the fire, for no one may escape, and see the result. The outward writing disappears, and there comes out: "A Child of God, Self-sacrificing, Tender-hearted, Forgiving." This is almost the same as the outside writing declared.

I. In this world, many persons pass for more than they really are. They read in such a way that they are praised for their liberality, when perhaps it is all selfishness with them; or they seem to be very liberal, but they make no real sacrifices from their abundant possessions, much of which may be ill-gotten. Others are very careful about going to church regularly, and seem to be very religious; but it is all a form with them, or is only done because it is considered a proper thing to do. Others are careful to have every one like them. They are much more careful about this than they are about what God thinks. All such persons are to be tested in the fire soon, and great surprises await them and their friends. It will be found that some who prophesied in Christ's name, preached for Him, and did many wonderfully religious things, and made many great sacrifices for Him, apparently, never knew Him.

II. There are others who will read better in that world than they have in this. Here they have been misjudged. The second paper, when held in the flame, revealed better things than were written on the outside; so it will be with many in the day when the work of all shall be tried by the fire. Like the widow who gave all her living to the Lord, they may give apparently so little to Him that they are not appreciated. But God knows their inward life, and that is the thing He cares about. Many are disliked because of their uncompromising stand against the sins of the world, and that is not, and never has been, enjoyed by those who practised the sins. Some have bitter enemies, who present them in a wrong light to the world, and they are misjudged all their life, in consequence. Hard things are often said about many good Christian people, and things that are untrue. Christ, and all His apostles, had to bear these things, and all His disciples now have to bear such reproaches to some extent. But the day when every secret thing is brought to judgment will make all these errors right.

III. The lives of some are such, that they are known by the world to be just about as they are within. Their lives are frank, and they have a good disposition, and they are sent by God on a mission of love. God has some that he sends as he did John the Baptist and Elijah, and some that have the message of the disciple John.

Be much more concerned about how your life reads inside, than you are about how your outward one reads. Your great temptation is to be careful about the outward reading, and forget the inward. The opinions of the world will soon vanish. In the "fiery trials" of life, and in those of death and the judgment, they will not count very much with you. Try to have your inner life right before God, and then let just as much of it as possible show out to the world. Remember that the writing, which is being done with an invisible pen and an invisible ink on your heart, will soon be brought to light, "whether it be good or whether it be evil."

XXIII.

THE WATCH.

I will praise thee; for I am fearfully and wonderfully made. Ps. 139:14.

[OBJECTS.—A watch that runs, and can be taken out of the case easily; one that has the mainspring either broken or gone; and a watch or clock that is in order, but will not keep good time, because it needs cleaning and oiling.]

I. "I am fearfully" made. That is, you, I, and every other person, are so delicately formed in body, mind, and spirit that the least little thing would injure us. We are so "fearfully" made that we cannot perform an action or gesture that does not apparently endanger some vein, artery, or muscle, the rupture of which would destroy our life or health. In this respect we are like this little watch. I cannot drop it, or open it and look at or touch its wheels, without being in danger of ruining it. It is so fearfully made that I must know about a watch to be enabled even to handle it without injuring it. When we look at the different parts of the body through a microscope they seem so delicately and fearfully made that it is a wonder that a boy can throw a stone, jump, or play football without rupturing some little membrane that would kill him.

II. Look into the works of a watch and see how wonderfully it is made. See all those little wheels, one going one way and another going another; some going fast and some slow; and all working together in just the right way to cause the hands to go round just fast enough to mark the time. And what an amount of work this little thing does! Few who carry a watch ever think of the unceasing labor it performs, under what would be considered shabby treatment of any other machinery. The main wheel of an ordinary American watch makes four revolutions in a day of twenty-four hours, or 1,460 in a year. The centre wheel goes around twenty-four times in a day, or 8,760 in a year. The third wheel makes 192 revolutions in a day, or 59,080 in a year; the fourth wheel 2,440 in a day, or 545,600 in a year; the fifth or escape wheel 12,960 in a day, or 4,728,200 in a year. The ticks or beats are 388,800 in a day, or 141,812,000 in a year. Truly the little watch is a wonderful machine, and able to perform an amazing amount of labor, if it is properly cared for.

So also every human body is a most wonderful machine. There is not a part of the body that is not most wonderful; even the smallest fibre of one of the muscles is a thing to admire and wonder at. The eye, ear, or even one drop of the blood, when looked at under the microscope, fills us with amazement. Then, too, how much labor any of these delicate parts of the body are able to accomplish! The heart works on day and night from infancy to old age, and never has a vacation, nor does it stop one moment for a little rest, but keeps working right on, sometimes for a hundred years. If the body is so wonderful, the mind and soul are more wonderful still. Every great discovery or achievement of man is the work of the mind. No wonder the Psalmist should say that he was wonderfully made!

III. A watch or clock is made to keep time, and to do it well. So you and I are fearfully and wonderfully made to praise God. The hills and trees praise Him; that is, they do all He made them to do, and so they bring honor to Him. So every creature on earth praises its Maker, by doing all that God intended it to do when He made it. We see this, and cannot help admiring the work God has wrought. But man is the only one of God's creatures that does not perform that for which God made him. Suppose one should make thousands of machines, and among them all a watch, and the watch were the only one that would not do what it was made to do. What would the maker of it do to it? Without doubt he would destroy it, and make something better. But God does not destroy us when we do not do as He intended us to. He is very patient and merciful with us.

Some watches do not keep time. Here is one that I cannot get to make one tick. I do not know just what is the difficulty with it, but I suspect that the mainspring is broken. In order that it may be made to keep time, it must be taken to a watchmaker. He would know in a moment just what the trouble is, and could easily make the needed repairs. So it is with many boys and girls: the mainspring of their soul is missing; that is, Christ in their heart. When they go to the Maker of their soul and body, and He repairs them, they have Christ within them, and then they praise God in all that they do. No one but God is able to make the needed repairs of the soul.

Sometimes the mainspring of a watch or clock is all right, and the wheels seem to be all in order, but the watch will run for a little time and then stop. Here is a clock that does just that way. It will run for a little time, and then stop. Sometimes it will run ten minutes, and again it will not run more than a minute. I suspect that the cause of this trouble is little particles of dust that have gotten into it, and then, too, it no doubt needs some oil on its wheels. That is just the way some boys and girls, and sometimes older people, praise God by their lives. The difficulty is that little sins get into their hearts and stop their living to His glory. A little lie, dishonesty, or an evil thought will do it as quickly as something greater. And then the wheels need often to be oiled. The Holy Spirit needs to dwell in the heart, in order that the life should be kept right.

IV. A watch that has been in the watchmaker's hand, and been repaired, will run without stopping and will keep good time. It does not make any difference whether it is in a gold case, a silver case, or in only a brass case. Any one whose soul is right, will praise God whether he is sick or well. It will make no difference either how homely or how nice looking he may be, or whether he is dressed in rags or in broadcloth: if his spirit is right he will praise God by his life and words. And he will never stop praising Him as long as he lives, and he will live forever; for Christ says, "Whosoever liveth and believeth in me shall never die." The soul of the Christian never dies. This watch which I hold in my hand keeps good time. (Call a boy or girl up and let him listen to it, and tell you what he hears.) I open the cases of the watch, and take the point of this penknife and touch a little screw that holds the works in the case, and out drop the works into my hand. (Let the boy listen again to the ticking of the watch as you hold it in your hand.) Now I will take the case of the watch and put it under my hat on the floor, and hold the works up in my right hand. There in the palm of my hand, it runs on as well as before.

This is just the way with a Christian. At a certain time in his life the dart of death comes into him, and touches that part which holds his soul and body together, and out goes the soul, all unharmed, and rests in the palm of God's hand, and there it praises Him forever. The body is put into the grave, and, at the resurrection, God will call it forth, and it and the soul will again be united, only it will be much more glorious than ever.

Let us say with the Psalmist, "I will praise thee; for I am fearfully and wonderfully made."

XXIV.

Paying for God's Benefits.

What shall I render unto the Lord for all his benefits toward me? I will take the cup of salvation, and call upon the name of the Lord. Ps. 116: 12, 13.

[OBJECTS.—Peroxide of iron and permanganate of potassium. When these are mixed in proper proportions, and water is poured upon them, it makes a liquid as red as blood. A quantity so small that it cannot be noticed in the bottom of a glass will, when the clear water is poured upon it, make the water appear to turn instantly to blood as fast as it is poured into the glass. You can tell, by trying, how much to put into the glass.

There are two ways in which this can be used to illustrate the text. One cup of water may represent the benefits I receive from God, or several little wine-glasses of water may represent the various benefits.]

I. What shall I render unto the Lord for all His benefits toward me?

1. Here is a small cup of clear water. Suppose we let this represent all the benefits of life. God gives us our life, food, strength, health, and the powers of our mind. What wonderful blessings these are!

2. Let this other little cup of water represent all the benefits of the world about us. Think of the sunshine, the rain, the fresh air, the birds, the flowers, and all the other beauties and benefits in the world around us that God has given us!

3. Consider this other cup as containing the blessings of the home. Some do not know much about the comforts of home. It is a great blessing to be in a land of homes, and where they are protected. A home is not only a place where we can find food, shelter, and rest, but a place in which we feel safe and natural. Any one who has a "home, sweet home" ought to feel that he has a great benefit from God.

4. We will let this other cup represent the benefits that come to us from our parents, our friends, our associates, our teachers, and all other persons who are a help to us.

When we think of all the great number of blessings that God has given to us, we ought to feel something as the Psalmist did when he said, "What shall I render unto the Lord for all his benefits toward me?" Suppose you look over all the benefits God has given you, and then say to yourself, "What shall I render unto the Lord for all these?" And then you begin to look around to see what you can give Him. You want to pay Him for them. How can you do it? You might think of the dearest thing you have, and say, "I will give Him that." But that could not pay Him, it matters not what it might be, whether it were money, friends, or even your life itself. Whatever you might think you would give Him is only what He has already given to you before. Every one of the blessings of your life belongs to God. He has let you have them to enjoy, and to think of paying Him for them by giving some of them back to Him is like trying to pay a friend for a large gift of money by taking a few cents from the pile and offering them to him as pay; or it is like taking a few drops of the water out of these small cups, that represent our benefits, and giving them to the one who let us have the whole, and saying to him, "Here, friend, are a few drops of water, to pay you for all this in the cups that you have given me." We cannot pay God for all His benefits toward us by giving Him anything. The other part of the text tells us how we can pay Him. It is by taking something more from Him.

As I take this large cup, which seems so

empty, so we can pay the Lord by taking from Him the cup of pardon or forgiveness. (The large glass has a *small* amount of the peroxide of iron and permanganate of potassium in it.) To most people the pardon of God is an empty thing, and it is indeed an empty thing, for it is His discharge of all claims against us because of our sins. Pardon is the cup of God's wrath given to us *empty*. We would have been compelled to drink the cup of His anger because of our sins; but Christ drank it Himself to the very dregs, and when it reaches us it is empty, and is the sweet cup of forgiveness.

Now, if I take all these benefits of God, represented by these little cups, and pour them into the cup of pardon, I see that there is a power in that cup to wonderfully change them. (As they are poured into the large cup they seem to be changed into blood.) That which before seemed an empty thing is now seen to have a power in it to change all that is put into it. That is just the way with the cup of salvation. When we take that cup, it seems to change the whole of the blessings of life. We then look at these things through eyes that are redeemed, and appreciate them with a heart that is washed, and we then realize that they come to us all for Christ's sake. A boy with Christian parents looks upon them very differently, after he has become a Christian, than he did before. Then he did not appreciate such parents, while now he is very thankful to God for such a great blessing. The cup of pardon has changed that blessing, so that it appears very different to him. After we have received the cup of salvation, every blessing enjoyed in life is seen to be bought by the precious blood of Christ. Every blessing is then colored by the blood.

Not only are the benefits of life made to seem very different to us after we take the cup of salvation, but those benefits themselves are so changed as to fill the cup of salvation itself. To the Christian, all things—and they are all blessings from God—are working together for his salvation. Every blessing, great or small, is poured into the cup of his salvation to make it complete and full. Whatever blessing God may give him, he takes with such a thankful heart that it is immediately transformed into a greater blessing still, by tending to save him.

So, if we take these benefits from God thankfully, and as given for Jesus' sake, they will help to fill our cup of salvation, till at last it will be full, and will run over with completeness. (As the last cup of water is poured into the large one, it causes the large one to run over.)

What shall you and I render unto the Lord for all His benefits toward us?

Take one more from Him, the cup of salvation, and, as they are received through that one cup of mercy to our soul, they are changed, and will at last fill the cup to overflowing.

We shall then be complete in Christ, through whom all these things have come to save us.

XXV.

THE STAR-FISH.

The fishes of the sea shall declare unto thee.
Job. 12:8.

[OBJECTS.—Star-fish. Several large and small ones if they can be obtained. Often they can be obtained from the sea-shore in their various stages of development or change.]

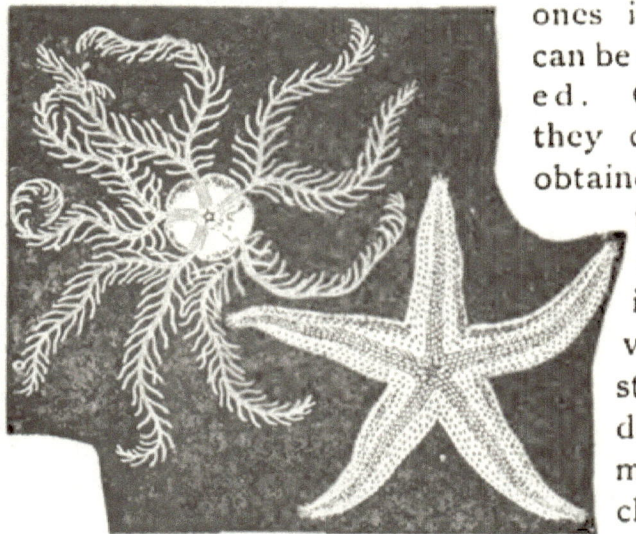

I. Though small, the star-fish is a most wonderful creature. He has 2,000 legs under the rays, in the seams. His mouth is in the centre, beneath. He has a greedy appetite—so greedy that he is called a walking stomach, and often eats bait that is set for fish, and so he is caught.

He has eyes in the end of each ray, which have from one to two hundred lenses.

"When a star-fish is spying after food, we observe it lift the ends of its pedicle-covered arms so that the downward-deflected eye there situated may obtain a good view of things in the neighborhood; and if in any direction, an object worth going after is discovered, we see the many hundreds of sucker-feet on the five arms push out in one and the same direction —a phenomenon that requires the presence of a very widely ramified nervous system, since every tactile pedicle needs its separate telegraph wire in order to be properly moved, and not always in the same direction, as, for example, when the animal wishes to perform a rotation about its own axis, for these comical animals sometimes do rotate about their axes, although our simple mind wonders why a Janus-head should want to turn around, these animals being able to look simultaneously in the four directions of the compass, and having still another eye for looking downward."

II. He has a most wonderful power of development. If through an accident, or for any reason, he loses one of his arms, he has the power to grow another.

In this he is like a boy or girl. There is a wonderful power for development that each person possesses. The most profound scholar has developed from a child who had little or no knowledge. The most devout Christian has developed from a state in which the kingdom of God in his heart was like a grain of mustard seed. So also the most wicked man in this world or the next has developed from a little innocent child. I wonder what you will develop into!

III. The star-fish has the power to break himself into pieces. If he be frightened or powerfully stimulated, he will often break off one or two of his rays. This is like the power for self-injury which every one possesses. Not only can he develop greatly, but can do himself great harm. "Do thyself no harm," said Paul to the jailor in Philippi. "Do thyself no harm," says the Holy Spirit to you.

IV. When he is growing you hardly know what he is going to make of himself. He is a mystery, and for a long time men did not know to what animal that little jelly substance belonged. He is merely a little jelly substance, with eight long legs, and with a network of lime upon his back. After a time he sinks to the bottom of the water, loses his legs, and the jelly substance is drawn up into his body.

Probably a child never came into a home that the parents did not look at him and think, "I wonder what kind of a man this little one will make!" We are constantly wondering, when we see boys and girls, what they are going to make of themselves. What kind of men and women will they become? We wonder all the more because we know that they have the power to be very good and useful, or to become very wicked and hurtful, to all about them.

V. This little animal is so complex in his make-up, and yet every part works in so much harmony with every other part, that one has said that it is composed of "five souls with but a single thought."

We are confronted with a fivefold Siamese monster, as it were, in which five separate persons are brought mentally under the same guidance, or where five minds have to pull, simultaneously, one rope. They could never defend themselves from their enemies, the cod or haddock, if it were not for this unity of action. They have no head, and yet one part never pulls one way and another part another way. If churches, families, and friends would observe this same union, they would be much better able to help themselves, and defend themselves against their enemies.

If a rubber band be slipped over one arm, all the others turn in and help the poor unfortunate one out of his trouble. The other arms bend themselves around, and with their rough surface push off the band. This is bearing one another's burdens.

If one of their arms be injured so as to endanger the whole life, they simply expel the unworthy or dead brother from their company. They have learned that it is not safe for them to keep company with those that are dead. He must be broken off, and they go at it and develop another. This is a good lesson for those inclined to keep company with those who are dead to God, and are willing to become nothing else. Death spreads unless it is cut off at once from our fellowship.

The little animal is able to walk because it has little sacks or suckers at the bottom of its feet, so that a little vacuum, or a space empty of air, is formed as it presses these down, and then draws up the foot. This enables it to cling to the most smooth surface, and to rocks when the waves are dashing powerfully upon them.

So if we have a little space of emptiness in our hearts, or where self does not reign, if we feel our nothingness, that is a little vacuum by which we can cling to the Rock of Ages in the severest storm, and be perfectly safe. The greatest danger with us is that we shall be full of self, and then have no clinging power. To be nothing before Him is to be very strong in Him.

XXVI.

The Bird's Nest.

Yea, the sparrow hath found an house, and the swallow a nest for herself, where she may lay her young, even thine altars, O Lord of hosts, my king, and my God. Ps. 84:3.

[Object.—A little bird's nest on a twig, with eggs in it.]

This was a little bird's home. Here it felt safe and happy. After a time the bird either left, or some one took the nest, and it has been given to me.

When this Psalm was written the birds were very kindly treated, and they built their nests almost anywhere they wanted to. They made them under the eaves of the houses, under the doorways, against the walls, and here it is said that they built them around the temple, and even under the edges of the altars. If they were not killed, it must have been because the people believed that God did not want any of his creatures harmed when they took refuge in His house.

I. If that be so, then the temple of God and the altars of God were good places for them to build, as no one would harm them there. How beautiful it is to think that even the little birds could be safe in the house of God; that there they could make their home, and rest in safety!

So the house of God is a good place for young and old now. It is a good Sabbath home, in which the soul can rest and worship God. Wandering birds have little rest. "No solid work can be expected from tramps, no religious growth and usefulness from those who wander about from church to church, sampling preachers." Birds on the wing lay no eggs and hatch no young. We should go so regularly to the house of God that it will be a home to us, and so regularly that we would feel lost and lonely when not there on a Sabbath.

II. Birds that built their nests under the edges of the altars are like all Christians—they are a type of worshippers. The altars stand for or are a type of Christ, the perfect man. And as the birds built their nests around the altars, so we are to take refuge in Christ. The nest there was a place of: 1. Security. How secure the little bird used to feel when it reached home after long flying about, and it could settle down into this little nest and rest! How secure one feels from every ruthless hand when he is in Christ! 2. The nest is a shelter from the storms. So Jesus is a shelter from the many storms of life. He breaks the force of them. 3. The nest is a covert to hide in. So is Christ. In Him we may hide from all the punishment that would fall upon us, because of the sins we have committed against God. He is the only safe hiding-place. Men try to find others, as Adam did, but they are no good. 4. The nest is a place to rest in. So is Christ. Rest for the soul cannot be found anywhere else. 5. The nest is a place to nestle in. There the little birds nestle, and listen to the storms raging and the winds blowing; and how comfortable and peaceful they feel! In Christ is a good place for His children to meet and enjoy His protection, and joy and rejoice while the storms are raging without.

The nest is an especially good place for the little birds. The Saviour is especially a good and safe place for the boys and girls. He is the only safe place, just as the nest is the only safe place for the little birds.

When the evening comes, the bird flies to her nest and rests. When the evening of life has come, and the day of life is past, how good it will be to go to the promised land of rest, and there enjoy the presence of God and His people forever! Blessed and happy are you if you go there! But God pity you if you have no possessions in that promised land, if you are homeless forever, having no place to rest, no place of security and peace, and that all because you would not seek your safety in Christ now. Let the birds that built their nests around God's temple and under the altars, teach you to seek Him as your home too, and do it now, for the storms will soon break upon you if you neglect.

XXVII.

HONEY.

Unto a land flowing with milk and honey. Ex. 3:8.

Sweeter also than honey and the honeycomb, Ps. 19:10 [or *droppings from the honeycomb*].

[OBJECTS.—A bottle of strained honey and a cake of honey. Show them, take a taste, or let another do so if you care to.]

This honey is like God's Word, and also like the Christian's home.

I. It cost great skill, planning, and labor to prepare it. We speak of the busy bee. How hard it works for the honey! How carefully it plans for the comb! This is true of the Word of God. How long it was being prepared, and how much labor and care were bestowed upon it!

But it is especially true of the Christian's Heavenly home—the land flowing with milk and honey. It would be beyond computation to determine the labor which that home has cost.

II. The honey is enjoyed by us, but at a

great sacrifice to the bee who wrought so hard and long for it. The bee was rich in honey, but, for us, goes with almost none.

What sacrifices God and His people made, that we might have the Word! Many lives have been given up, that we might have it in our own tongue to read!

What sacrifices Christ made that we might have the joy of Heaven! He who was rich gave up all, that we might be rich. If you reach Heaven, it will be because One has made great sacrifices, that you might do so. If you miss it, He has made the sacrifice, as far as you are concerned, all for nothing.

III. In their sweetness the Word of God and Heaven are like honey. But each one must taste for himself, or all will be in vain. I cannot eat the honey for you. "Oh, taste and see."

XXVIII.

The Prism.

Let your light so shine before men, that they may see your good works, and glorify your Father which is in heaven. Matt. 5 : 16.

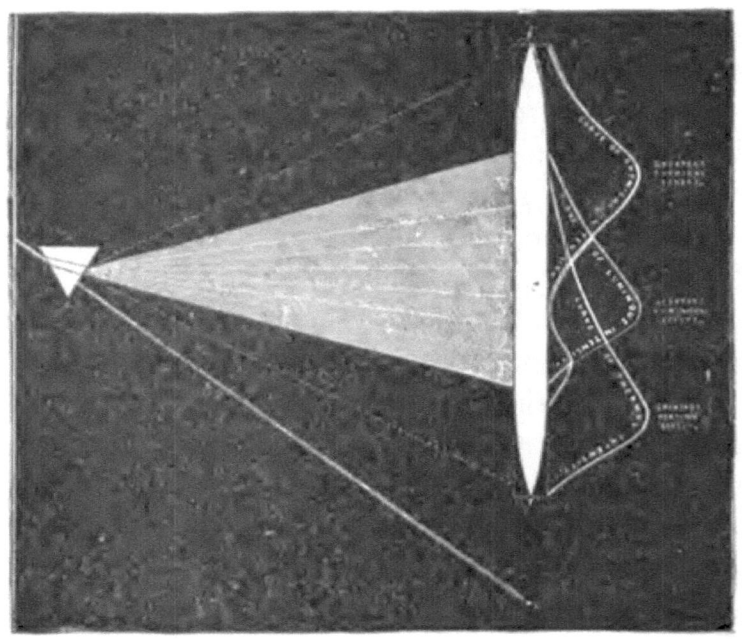

[OBJECT. — A prism. If possible let a ray of sunlight shine through it.]

A ray of sunlight is a wonder. No object can be exposed to it without undergoing a change. It has life-giving properties, and at the same time it has the power of consuming many things it falls upon. It destroys decayed matter and purifies the atmosphere. It is also a thing of beauty. But to see just how beautiful it is, one must let it shine through a prism. As it is then separated into the different parts of which it is composed, you behold all the colors of the rainbow. And by combining these colors, every beautiful color in the world is made. These colors are:

1. Violet; 2. Indigo; 3. Blue; 4. Green; 5. Yellow; 6. Orange; 7. Red.

Just so the light which is shed by the Holy Spirit is most wonderful. No one can come under the power of His light without being changed. He has a life-giving, and also a consuming, power.

But to see the beauty of the light He sheds, one must behold it as it shines through the heart of a sinner. As He shines into the heart, the light comes out in most beautiful colors in the daily life. Here are some of those beautiful colors: 1, Love; 2, joy; 3, peace; 4, longsuffering; 5, gentleness; 6, goodness; 7, faith; 8, meekness; 9, temperance.

As the sunlight shining through the prism always shows the seven primary colors mentioned above, so the Holy Spirit shining through any heart, always shows the nine beautiful graces just mentioned. These may be called the nine primary graces of every true Christian.

As every beautiful thing in the world is produced by the combination of the seven primary colors of sunlight, so every beautiful thing that is said, done, or thought in this world is the result of combining these nine primary graces.

Ask God to shine into your heart; and it matters not how sinful it may be, it will be manifest in a beautiful life now, and it will grow more and more beautiful till in the Heavenly world it will be perfectly beautiful.

XXIX.

IRON SHARPENING IRON.

Iron sharpeneth iron; so a man sharpeneth the countenance of his friend. Prov. 27 : 17.

[OBJECTS.—A common steel used to sharpen knives, and a long carving-knife. Sharpen the knife on the steel.]

These are both made from iron, and yet one sharpens the other.

I. It says in the text that the countenance is sharpened. You sharpen the mind or spirit, and that sharpens the face. The wisdom shows in the countenance. "Countenance" is from a verb which means "to turn about." "Friend" is from a verb meaning "to feed." One is turned about when in a wrong way, and is fed at the same time, by the wise counsel of a friend.

II. The steel and knife are more or less alike —they are made from the same material. So friends, to be helpful to each other, must be more or less alike. They must be similar in make-up, or have similar experiences, or have something in common. Afflicted souls best comfort those who are afflicted; mourners the mourning ones; and boys can greatly help boys.

III. There must be a proper contact between the knife and steel. So there must be right and proper associations in life, in order not to injure rather than benefit. It will not do to hack the knife on every kind of an iron.

VI. There is more or less roughness in the steel; that does the sharpening. So if one is to be truly benefited by a friend, he must expect more or less harshness or friction. It is not pleasant to be warned of one's faults, and sometimes it is very unpleasant. The more the knife needs sharpening, the more of the nicks and edges must be taken off; and this means friction.

But, as the sharpening progresses, it removes the rough edge of the knife, and makes both the knife and steel brighter. Both friends are made brighter by the sharpening process.

V. One cuts better, but it is at the expense of the other, which is being worn out by the process. If a friend is made better by the advice and counsel of his friend, it often costs the one who does the sharpening more than it does the one who receives it. It is no easy task to be a true friend.

VI. When the steel is new, it rakes very hard in the work of sharpening, and it becomes less and less harsh as it grows older at the business. Friends who are new at reproof and advice are often very profuse with it, and are regardless of how harsh their words may be. But as they grow older and have more experience, they become softened. They have more tenderness and charity. It is true they do not sharpen so quickly as when it is done roughly, but it is done with less injury to the feelings. Remember it is not necessary to wound, to sharpen the countenance of a friend.

VII. Both the knife and steel must be in the master's hand. They must not be in the hand of an inexperienced person or a child, to receive benefit. Hacking on the steel by a novice will not do. If friendships in this world are to be of mutual benefit, they must be formed in Christ. The friends must be in the hands of the Master. We often think we are wise enough to judge who ought to be our friends and companions. Associations that are to be formed with benefit to the parties forming them, must be under the direction of Christ. He alone can make you a benefit to others, or they to you.

XXX.

A Yellow Jacket's Nest or a Wasp's Nest.

Consider her ways and be wise. Prov. 6:6.

Hold up the nest.  This is an evidence of the wisdom of the wasp.

I. It shows what a little wasp can do when it works peaceably with other wasps. It shows unity of aim or object — all trying to do one thing. It is a lesson on the harmony of action.

Love one another and work one with another. Don't sting one another with bitter sayings or looks.

II. It shows the wisdom of providing, for the future, a home and food.

1. Some boys and girls, and older people too, live only for the present. They save nothing, but use all that they get. They want to be like rich people. Save and be not stingy. Save for an education, for a home, that you

may have a place for those who have no home.

2. "Lay up for yourselves treasures in heaven, where neither moth nor rust doth corrupt." "I go to prepare a place for you." "Provide for the future," say the ants and the bees. And so says the Word of God.

XXXI.

Sand.

Treasures hid in the sand.   Deut. 33 : 19.

[Object.—A box or glass jar of sand.]

The lessons learned are treasures.

I. Sand is made of very small stones. The grain of sand is just as much a stone as a large rock, only it is smaller.

Children are small men and women.

II. One can sit in the sand by the seashore, and not get soiled. It is clean.

Little children are so. You do not become soiled by being among them. It is from the older ones that our mind and soul are soiled.

III. Sand is small, but it binds together all the houses in every great city like this, when it is mixed with lime in the mortar. It is also used to bind the engine to the track, so that it can draw the heavily loaded train. So children very often bind homes together. Father and mother work together better for the children's sake, and they are better able to draw the heavy loads in life, because of their children.

IV. The grains of sand combined, keep old ocean back. God has placed the sand by the sea for a bound of the sea (Jer. 5:22). One grain could do nothing.

This teaches us the power of sticking together, or unity, even among little children. What a power for good when they love one another, especially those in the same family!

V. One grain can do much harm when out of its proper place. In a watch it stops it; in an eye it ruins it.

So a child who frequents saloons, or goes with evil companions, will soon become so that he will do great harm to every right-minded boy or girl with whom he associates. He is like a grain of sand in a watch.

VI. When sand is put into a furnace, with other materials, and melted, it makes glass, clear as crystal. Children who receive the Holy Spirit into their hearts, are moulded into pure and holy beings. Under His power, their characters become clear, beautiful, and useful.

VII. When sand is transformed or made over, it is very useful in giving stability or strength to great things. It is that in the stalks of grain, quills of feathers, and bamboo which gives them strength. How much spiritual strength there is in a boy or girl who has been converted! He is a power for good even among greater ones, and is a means of encouragement and strength to them.

VIII. Sand shows us how God thinks of us.

"How precious also are thy thoughts unto me, O God! how great is the sum of them! If I should count them, they are more in number than the sand" (Ps. 139: 17, 18).

So children who are small and helpless, often teach their parents how He loves and cares for them. Many valuable lessons on the fatherhood of God are first learned when a little child comes into the home.

Even the small sand can do much good, it is of great value, and can be made a thing of beauty and usefulness. It can also do great harm.

Strive, then, to be good and useful, rather than great.

XXXII.

NEW WINE AND OLD BOTTLES.

And no man putteth new wine into old bottles; else the new wine will burst the bottles, and be spilled, and the bottles shall perish. But new wine must be put into new bottles; and both are preserved. No man also having drunk old wine straightway desireth new; for he saith, The old is better. Luke 5 : 37–39.

[OBJECT.—An old water-bag or skin such as is used in Palestine.]

See the reading in Revised Version, and explain the meaning by showing the wine-skin.

The reason for that which Christ tells us in the text, is that new wine begins to grow or expand at the time of fermentation, and the old dried skin would crack and break, and all be spilled. But a new wine-skin, one just taken off the back of an animal, is green or tough, and is elastic; so, as it stretches, it can make room for the expansion of the wine, and so both are preserved.

Jesus uses this as an illustration, primarily, of the impossibility of putting the new spirit of divine life given by Him, into the Old Testament forms and ceremonies. So when He came, He did not go first to the religious teachers, the Pharisees and rulers in the church at that time. He knew that they were fixed in their opinions of what was right and proper, and He could not change them to believe in the real true way God's grace should come to the world. So He chose fishermen and such persons to be His disciples, and through whom to first give His gospel. They were not prejudiced. They were not fixed in their views. Their lives could expand as the new spirit of life which was in them expanded.

This new life was not, either, to be put into the same old forms and ceremonies which had been used so long. It was to be put into something more appropriate to its newness. Some seem to think that the gospel of Christ is to be in the same old wine-skins of formality that existed for so many centuries, but they are mistaken. There is no life in forms and ceremonies. Some boys and girls think they would hardly be saved if they were not confirmed. There is no saving work about that. That cannot save, any more than any other form can save. Partaking of the communion cannot save one. These things, at most, are the wine-skins. If the new wine of the kingdom of Heaven is not already within, the outward show does no good. If one has just certain forms and ceremonies, and he always does his religious work just according to these prescribed rules, there is no chance for him to let the grace in his heart expand or grow. He is, as we say, in the rut. The new wine is in the old skin, and the old skin will crack and break when the wine expands.

So again, we learn that the new spiritual life of Christ is not to be put into our old life. It is to be put into a new heart given to us. The old heart is not made over, either. It is a new heart, and the Spirit of Christ lives in that new heart, or new nature if you wish to call it that; and so then our whole life is new.

A new Spirit and a new heart, and an entirely new life, is the result.

So your being a Christian is not merely to do better than you are doing, or have done. It is being a new boy or a new girl in Christ. He gives you that new heart, and puts His Spirit into you, which to you is a new life.

Remember three things about this wine-skin:

First.—Come to the Bible, not having your mind all made up what is right to believe and do, and determined you will not change it, but come willing to be taught and have all your ideas changed, if they are not like what the

Bible teaches. Then you will be like the new wine-skin to new wine—you can expand.

Second.—Don't think that forms and ceremonies are religion, and that if you are a Christian you can be one only as you use them. That would make you narrow. If you have the new life, it will expand beyond all these things. You will not depend upon them.

Third.—Remember that the new spiritual life of Christ is to be in a new heart, and your life is to be new, if you become a true Christian.

New wine must be put into new wine-skins.

XXXIII.

THE KEY OF DAVID.

These things saith he that . . . hath the key of David. Rev. 3: 7.

[OBJECTS.—Many locks and keys, large ones, small ones, padlocks, rusty ones, bright ones, brass and iron ones, the greater the variety the better.]

Jesus is the One who has the key of David. The key of David is the key by which he opens his house. It shows our Lord's own supreme power in the kingdom of God. He is the one who has the power to unlock the kingdom of Heaven, and let souls in. No man, aside from His power, can do this. He alone unlocks the kingdom to us sinners. But it is not the kingdom that needs to be unlocked, it is our hearts. So He unlocks the kingdom to us by unlocking our hearts.

Our hearts are just like these locks. The small ones with the small spring inside are children or young people, and the large ones with heavy springs and large bolts are older persons. The rusty ones are the persons who have, either by neglect or sin, come nearer to ruin and uselessness than others.

No one key will fit any two of these locks, which may teach us that no two of us are just alike. They differ in age, size, and make, and so do we. Here are two that look just alike, and yet the key for one will not fit the other. That is just the way with us; we may look alike, and seem to be alike, and yet we are very different, and have to have a key to fit into our soul entirely different from that which fits any other.

I. Jesus is the key of David, in that He knows the way to every heart. You may be small and young, like this little lock, and yet Jesus knows the way into your heart. You may be large and old, like this very large lock, or you may be rusty with many sins and neglect of care or use, and still Jesus knows the way into your heart. There is no kind of a lock, that has an entrance, which this Key does not know the way into.

II. The Saviour knows how also to unlock every heart that can be unlocked. He knows how to bring out all the powers of every soul. He can use the means that will make every one do his best, and that is doing all God intended that one to do when He created him. See how souls that give themselves up to Jesus are made to grow! See how the powers of their soul, that before were unknown, are brought out and made perfect! Every true Christian shows this, and more and more as he comes more completely under the power of Jesus.

III. He knows too, how to make every rusty lock work smoothly. Just as I pour some oil into this rusty lock, which works so hard, and it works much more easily, so Jesus pours the oil of His grace into the soul of the worst sinner, and he works as well as any. One great trouble with some locks is that they are rusty inside and so work hard. So it is with many Christians: they are rusty inside, and need more of the oil which Jesus can pour into their souls.

IV. Every lock has different kinds of springs inside, and so each one needs a different kind of a key. So every soul has different longings, or troubles. But Jesus is the key that can touch every spring of each soul. There is not another who has this power, which He has. To the young, to the old, to the sick, to the well, to the rich, to the poor, to the living, to the dying, to the happy, to the sad, to the tempted, to the weak or sinful soul, Jesus has just that which each one feels in need of. He so touches every spring of each soul that all the wants are met. He satisfies every want. Those who have wandered over the world in search of that which would satisfy, and have not found it, if they come to Him, are so satisfied that their joy knows no bounds.

There are other keys, such as crooked, rusty nails or weak, bent pins, but they are little good after all. Jesus is the only one who can touch every spring of each needy soul.

XXXIV.

Testing by the Thermometer.

"Let us search and try our ways." Lam. 3:40.

[Objects.—An ordinary weather thermometer and a physician's thermometer.]

I. This weather thermometer tells how hot or cold the atmosphere is. Plants or animals die if it is too hot or too cold. So let us try our atmosphere, our surroundings, our associates, those whom we make our friends. Bad company is bad atmosphere. Go in the company of those who are cold and dead to God, and you will become cold and dead to Him yourself. Bad books are also a very bad atmosphere. Look out that you do not get poisoned in this way!

II. The physician's thermometer. Put this into your mouth, and leave it for a time, and it will tell how hot or cold you are—if the fire of life is burning too low or too fast. The other was to try the atmosphere, this one is to try the person himself. Try your temperature. 1. By what comes out of the mouth, we may try how our real life, God's fire, is burning within. Our words tell what our spiritual temperature is. 2. Spiritual inactivity is also a test of the temperature. One freezing in the snow wants to lie down and sleep, but it is only because he is so cold, his temperature is so low, that he wants to be inactive, which means death. 3. God's Word is the best tester of our temperature. Look often into that, and see how your temperature reads, and you will be on the safe side. Some, like Jehu, are all zeal and no faith or love. Zeal alone is a fire which soon burns up the life; it is a fever which by itself will make one delirious; cause him to lose his head. But some are so cold that they are dying. They have so little faith and love, they are dying from heart failure.

Since our temperature is governed by the atmosphere we are in, let us get into, and keep into, Jesus' company. Feed your fire by the fire of the Holy Spirit, and it will be safe and right.

XXXV.

The Fiery Darts.

And above all, taking the shield of faith, wherewith ye shall be able to quench all the fiery darts of the wicked (one). Eph. 6 : 16.

[OBJECTS.—Fire grenades, concealed till you wish to use them.]

Refer to the great fire in Chicago in 1871, or to some other great fire. How many millions of property were destroyed! And how many lives lost! And  how many were made poor! But if you or I had been there when it first started, we could have easily put it out in a moment. Here is what we could have done it with (showing the extinguisher). When this is thrown into a flame, it creates a gas in which the flame cannot live. But the fire must be taken when it begins. It is then very easy to put it out.

There are other fires than those that burn up buildings and make people homeless. They are the fires that are kindled in the soul, and that consume it. Satan is the author of these fires. He shoots his flaming arrows into the soul, just as in olden times in war, they used to shoot flaming arrows over the walls into cities to consume them. So God's Word warns us against these fiery darts or arrows of Satan. Here are some of the darts he shoots into the soul:

I. Unbelief in God and His Word. Nearly every fire of the soul begins right here. It is usually only a spark, but will flame up rapidly if you give it a chance.

II. Selfishness is another dart. Satan gives us all sorts of reasons why we should be selfish, and they look so plausible too; but he only intends to set the soul on fire by this sin.

III. Laziness, spiritual and physical, is another dart. The desire for ease in religious things, or comforts of the body or daily life, are very powerful darts. Some one has said that laziness is the original sin. It certainly is very prevalent.

IV. Deception is another dart. The temptation is usually at first, to deceive in very small and trifling matters. Satan knows that a big fire can be kindled from this if it is only allowed in the soul.

V. Procrastinating duty to pray, read the Bible, or the like. The ruin of the soul often begins with this putting off a duty.

If you will notice these darts, you will see that none of them are usually considered to be very dangerous. But they are just the kind the enemy of our soul loves to shoot. He knows they will kindle a big fire just as well as a mighty flaming dart, and they do not attract so much attention, and so are not so liable to be put out by us.

But every one should have his fire grenade always ready, and then he is safe. The text tells us what that grenade is—"the shield of faith." It is trust in Jesus, or confidence in the Saviour. It is believing that God always and everywhere tells the truth. It is believing Him so thoroughly that you flee to Him for safety, and try to get every one else to do the same. If one reads what He says, and believes it, he will not yield to any of Satan's temptations to live in sin. There is nothing in the way of fiery darts that this trust or confidence in Christ will not quench instantly, if you only give it a trial. So, withal, take the shield of faith.

XXXVI.

Stony Hearts.

Harden not your hearts.   Heb. 3 : 15.

[OBJECTS.—Some soft clay and a brick, or some clay stone having some tracks of insects or fossils in it, if possible.]

I. This stone was once soft like this clay. Just so are the hearts of you boys and girls. You cannot look on cruel things, or do wicked deeds.

II. It became hard very gradually, and all unnoticed. Age hardened it. You will grow harder as you become older, and especially if you are not a Christian. Soil that is left, gradually grows hard, till at last it seems baked. So will your soul, if it be not cultivated for God.

III. It is now so hard that it is permanent or fixed. So you are becoming just like this rock, fixed or permanent, either fixed in sin or holiness. You are growing to be permanently either good or bad.

IV. There are some little tracks which the little insects left here when this stone was soft clay. There they crawled and left their tracks.

So when you are old you will show the tracks that are being made upon your soul now. Are they tracks of evil thoughts, vile language, bad books, bad associates, and sinful deeds? Or are they going to be the marks of a good, pure, Christian life?

V. This hard stone cannot make itself soft again. But acid can make it tender, or, it could be crushed under the hammer.

You cannot make your own heart tender, but the Holy Spirit can melt it, and keep it tender. If He does not do it now, soon your heart will be crushed under the hammer of God's justice.

Pray for the Holy Spirit to come into your heart to make it tender toward God, and against sinning. "Harden not your heart" by refusing to let Him into your soul.

XXXVII.

The Anchor.

Which hope we have as an anchor of the soul, both sure and steadfast, and which entereth into that within the veil. Heb. 6: 19.

[OBJECT.—A small anchor and chain. One that is used to anchor sail-boats is a good size.]

The Christian's hope is like an anchor. No ship is complete without an anchor.

I. The anchor is used to keep the ship or boat steady. So hope in God's Word of truth holds the soul from being driven by the winds of doubt and sin.

II. The anchor is needed most in storms. The storms will come to every one in life, and then we need an anchor, and there is none like hope in Christ. It is the only one that will hold in death.

III. Anchors go down under the water. They are of no use if they only lie upon deck. Ours goes up into Heaven, and is in Christ.

IV. Ships often drag their anchors when in a storm, for they are only in the soft mud.

Sometimes professed Christians seem to drag their anchor, and are driven on to the rocks, but it is only because they have the anchor in mud, and not in Christ. If it is in Him it is "both sure and steadfast."

V. Anchors are used to "kedge up" with; that is, wind the ship into port. The anchor is thrown into a good solid place, and then the anchor chain is gradually wound around a windlass, and it draws the ship up to the anchor. So the Christian's anchor is used to "kedge up" to Heaven with.

No hope is good that is not born of the Holy Spirit. Let Him get hold of the chain with you, and you will not let go. The Holy Spirit at one end, in the heart, and the anchor in Christ in Heaven, and there is safety. There is no safety but this. You would loose your grip on the chain in the first storm, but the Holy Spirit, never!

XXXVIII.

Growth of the Power of Sin.

Now, therefore, be ye not mockers, lest your bands be made strong. Isa. 28 : 22.

[OBJECTS.—Call a boy up to help you preach the sermon. Have a spool of strong white cotton thread. Have him put his hands down by his sides, and put one or two threads about his arms, and ask him if he can break it. This he can do with the utmost ease. It may please him and others, to think of tying him with a thread or two. Put four or five threads about him, and they do not break quite so easily. While doing this you can be talking of the way some make light of the power of sin. Then wind twenty-five or thirty about him, and see if he can break them. He probably cannot. You can tell by having some one try it on yourself before you try it on a boy. When you have him bound up so that he cannot move, you can tell him that this is just the way little sins will bind his soul if he commit them. Then you can show some larger cords, and state that sins do not always remain small like the thread, although they keep on fastening themselves around the soul. Then show a small chain, and finally a large log chain, and wrap it around him a moment to illustrate the way Satan binds the soul with sins Then take a large pair of shears and cut the threads very quickly so that he is free again.]

In sin there are three steps.

I. The first is unthinking security, and so there is a tendency to make light of the power of sin—it is thought of as the boy thought of one or two threads about his arms. It is not thought worth effort to break them, they are so small and weak. This is the "mocking" period in the text. But the sins continually grow stronger, and lead to others.

II. The second stage in sin, is a state of conscious discord between one's self and God. He chafes against his chains, and as Samson groaned in his prison, he longs to be free from his servitude. This is like the boy struggling when he had thrity or more threads wound about him. The struggles are soon found to be in vain, and the soul falls deeper.

III. The third stage of sin, namely, obduracy or insensibility. There is a callousness on the soul as the result of persevering in the neglect of conscience. Here all struggles cease. The soul is bound with chains. When the boy saw he could not break the threads, and then ropes and chains were put around him, he utterly despaired of breaking them. It is just so with the soul steeped in sin. It sinks into utter indifference or despair.

IV. But Christ can cut the cords that bind. Just as in a moment the cords were cut from this boy, so in a moment Christ can set the soul free. This is why He came to this world. In Isa. 61:1 it says He came "to proclaim liberty to the captives, and the opening of the prison to them that are bound," and in Luke 4:18 He quotes these very words as applying to Himself. We know He did not open Roman prisons and let the prisoners out, and it must refer to souls that are imprisoned, and He is the strong man to set them free.

This cutting of cords that bind, is all done by Christ through the Spirit, and not by self-struggles. When Samson was bound with cords by the Philistines and they shouted against him, the Spirit of the Lord came mightily upon him, and the cords that were upon his arms became as flax that was burnt with the fire and his bands loosed from off his hands.

Many Christians are bound by the cords of sin, and have little happiness and less freedom.

But it is all useless, for all these things would melt in a moment in the presence of the Holy Spirit.

Let no one mock at sin, lest his bands become stronger, and let every hampered soul turn fully to Christ, and have the bliss of the free sons of God. And then stand fast in the liberty wherewith Christ hath made us free, and be not entangled again with the yoke of bondage.

XXXIX.

The Pedometer.

Walk worthy of the vocation wherewith ye are called. Eph. 4: 1.

Thou compassest my path and my lying down, and art acquainted with all my ways. Ps. 139: 3.

[OBJECT.—A pedometer. One can be purchased, or loaned for the occasion.]

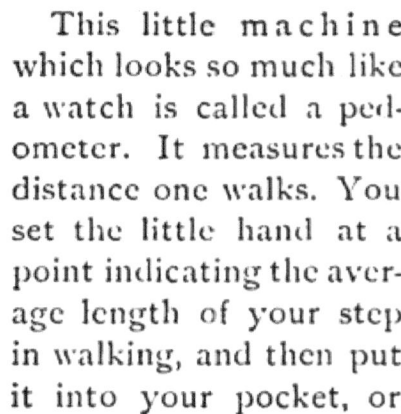

This little machine which looks so much like a watch is called a pedometer. It measures the distance one walks. You set the little hand at a point indicating the average length of your step in walking, and then put it into your pocket, or fasten it upright on a belt, and every step you take the hand registers it, and you tell by the figures how far you have gone.

We are taught by the first text that the way we live in this world is called our walk. If we live right, our walk is a good one; while if we live a sinful life, our walk is an evil one.

By the second text we are told that God holds a pedometer of our walk in life.

I. This little thing tells just how far we have gone while walking. It may say you have walked ten miles since you put it on. It now says that I have walked one and one-quarter miles since I put it into my pocket. You cannot tell how far you have gone in life. You know how old you are, but you do not know how near you may be to the end of your life. Neither can any one tell just how far you may be in sin, or how far you have gone in your knowledge of Jesus, but God knows exactly. He keeps a register of all.

II. This registers every step, whether it be one of full length, or whether it be a false one. The hand moves because of the jars of the body; so any false step is registered as well as the most perfect one.

Just so every act of yours is registered. It may have been a good one, or it may have been an evil one. It is registered in the earth, the air, the light, on your body and mind; and God sees and keeps a register of all.

III. This little machine cannot tell where you walk, whether into a saloon, a church, or in the street. It would be a good thing sometimes if parents had a pedometer that would tell where their children go. Old people too, would often be ashamed to have such a thing as that tell on them. But God keeps a record of just *where* you go, and He never forgets.

IV. You cannot tell either by this, with *whom* you walk. What a tale such an instrument would tell if it could say just what company one keeps, and what he says! That cannot be known now, but will be known soon. All these secrets will be out in that day, when we stand before God.

V. You can turn this instrument upside down, and then it cannot register. You cannot turn God's registering machine upside down. Men try in life to defeat all His plans, and often succeed partially in covering up their sins for a time, but still God's register is marking down the deeds. You may think you are alone, and no one sees or hears; but if your ears were only a little sharper you could hear the tick, tick of God's registering machine, and if your eyes were a little clearer you could see the hand move one point more, as each sin is committed.

VI. This is the registering time, but soon the reading time will come when everybody shall see just how you have lived and thought; so be very careful *how* you walk in life, and *where* you walk, and with *whom* you walk.

If you will walk hand in hand with the Saviour, you shall have nothing to fear, and you will "walk worthy of the vocation wherewith ye are called."

XL.

Life and Life-like.

He that hath the Son, hath life; and he that hath not the Son of God, hath not life. I. John 5 : 12.

[Objects.—Bust of Shakespeare or anything similar. A hideous little image or god.]

This is a bust of Shakespeare. It looks something as he looked when he was alive. But there is a great difference between this and Shakespeare. He was a living person, and this is dead, and always will be. It has no life in it—no spirit. It is just as dead as this god (or any other object), although it looks much better. If it were marble, or bronze, or even gold, it would be dead just the same. However beautiful it might be, would make no difference. So long as it has no spirit in it, it is dead.

This is what the text means. All who have the Spirit of Jesus, have life; and all who have Him not, have not life.

I. You may be beautiful in looks and in acts, and yet not have life. You may act just as a Christian does, as one who has spiritual life, and not have life. Wax men and women make the same motions that living men and women do. The actions of wax men cannot make them alive. Your doing good things, and your being good, cannot make you a Christian. You must have the Spirit of life given you by the Saviour.

II. If you have the Son, you have life. To have anything is to own it, to possess it. Those who possess things, have different places to keep them. A man has money, and he keeps it in the bank. A boy has a knife, and he keeps it in his pocket. He has a mother, and she is in the home. So if you have the Son, you will have a place for Him, a home, and that home is your heart. He says: "Behold, I stand at the door, and knock: if any man hear my voice, and open the door, I will come in to him, and will sup with him, and he with me."

You may be good, and even say your prayers, and yet not have spiritual life, not be a Christian. But if you pray Jesus to come into your heart, He will come in, and then you will have life forever.

III. It is no sign that one is a Christian because he never did anything very bad. If not being or doing anything bad could make one a Christian, then this image would be a better

Christian than any one of us, for it has never done the least wrong thing. You are a Christian—you have life—if you have the Son; but you have not life—you are not a Christian—if you have not the Son of God.

IV. Doing the best one can does not make him a Christain; this image has always done the very best it could, but that has made no difference with it—it is as dead as ever, there is no life in it. Doing nothing or doing everything does not make one a Christian, but having the Son makes him one, for he then has life.

XLI.

Masks.

For nothing is secret that shall not be made manifest; neither anything hid that shall not be known and come abroad. Luke 8 : 17.

[Object.—A mask or false face. Put it on your face to let the boys and girls see how it changes your looks.]

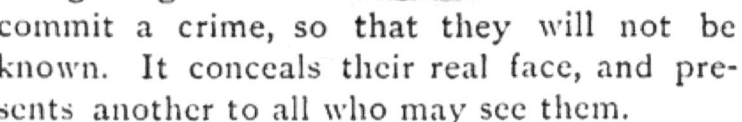

A mask is something that men sometimes put on their face when they are going to commit a crime, so that they will not be known. It conceals their real face, and presents another to all who may see them.

Such masks usually make the persons wearing them look much worse than they do when their natural face is seen. But this is not the case with all masks that are worn. Indeed, there are many worn to cover wicked hearts, and bad deeds, that are very fine looking. It is just as if one who is very homely in the face should go and buy a fine false face, and put it on to make himself nice looking.

See what a fine-looking mask Judas wore, when he went up to Jesus, and said, "Hail, master," and kissed Him. He looked very different in that act than he really looked within.

What a fine-looking mask Joab wore when he met Amasa, and made believe he was going to kiss his friend Amasa, and he said, "Art thou in health, my brother?" and stabbed him with his left hand.

Jacob wore a mask when he went in and stole the blessing away from his brother Esau. Herod wore a mask when he said he wanted to know where the child Jesus was, that he might go and worship Him. Ananias and Sapphira wore a mask when they tried to keep back a part of the price of the possessions they had sold.

Many times nowadays men wear masks to conceal their wicked deeds. Sometimes they become members of churches, so that others will think they are very good. Sometimes they are very benevolent, or seem greatly interested in Christian work, but it is only for a mask to deceive people. Sometimes a young man who is vile and bad, seems very religious and pure, so that he can get some fine young lady to marry him. He is wearing a mask, and she does not know it.

Many of those who are now wearing masks to conceal great hideousness, began by wearing masks to cover very small things. It may have been to conceal a little falsehood, or to take some little thing that did not belong to them; or seem very nice and kind when out in company, or at church, when at home they were very disagreeable; or to appear very glad to see some acquaintance, when in reality they were not glad at all to see him. Often people put on a mask by seeming very pleasant to one's face, and then talking against him when he is not around. Hatred of some one in the heart, or jealousy at some one's prosperity, are often the cause of masks that are worn by those who seem to be very good people.

The following is always true. Any one who puts a little mask on to hide a little spot now, will soon have to put a big mask on to hide a big spot, till at last it will be hideous under the mask.

The text says there is a time coming when all masks will be torn off. Judas had his torn off, and so did the other persons I mentioned. Many have them torn off in this life. But some men do not have them torn off till after they die. Then it may be discovered that they were defaulters, or something of the kind.

Nothing is secret that shall not be made manifest in the other world. All the great masks, and all the small masks, will be torn off then. Some sins that men have committed, and have forgotten all about, will then come to light.

Remember this: " He that covereth his sins shall not prosper; but whoso confesseth and forsaketh them shall have mercy." It is much better to have them all uncovered, or confess them here, and have them forgiven, than it is to have them concealed in this life, and then have God uncover them in the Judgment, and punish them.

XLII.

The Veil.

But their minds were blinded: for until this day remaineth the same vail untaken away in the reading of the old testament; which vail is done away in Christ. II. Cor. 3 : 14.

[OBJECT.—An ordinary large dark veil. As it is used to illustrate the growing darkness which covers the heart of one who sins, it can be folded over at each point.]

I. The meaning of the text is, that when the Israelites sinned, it darkened their minds to the power of sin, so that they could not so well understand the terribleness of sin, nor could they so well understand the Bible. They continued to sin, and their blindness of heart increased, till they could not understand the true nature of God's truth at all.

II. So sin puts a veil over one's eyes or heart now.

If a boy lies, it puts a little veil over his eyes, so that a lie does not seem so terrible to him as it did before. Neither can he see the nature of truth quite so well.

If he goes on, and uses profane language, the veil thickens, just as I fold this one. If he steals something, the veil over his heart becomes thicker still.

Then, perhaps evil thoughts make the veil thicker, and then the Saviour is rejected, and the veil is doubled again; and as the one continues to sin, it at last becomes so thick that not a ray of light can get through. Then the soul is in utter darkness, having been blinded by sin, and the lost one does not know where he is going. He is like a blind person following a blind guide, for his heart is his guide, and it is blinded. His soul is just like my eyes with this thick veil over them—utterly blinded.

III. But the text says the veil is done away when one turns to Christ. If one truly turns to Him, the veil is removed in a moment, just as I remove this veil from my eyes. Then the soul sees clearly, and not till then.

XLIII.

The Caught Mice.

A prudent man foreseeth the evil, and hideth himself; but the simple pass on, and are punished. Prov. 22: 3.

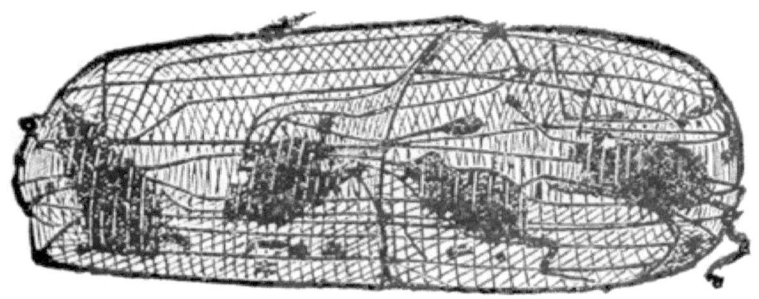

[OBJECTS.—A mouse-trap, and possibly a toy mouse. Mice as they were caught in the trap were used when this sermon was preached.]

I. The wise one is looking out for the evil before it comes. The foolish one sees it after it has come. Who could not see it then?

II. The prudent one learns from the experiences of others; the foolish one only from his own experience.

III. The prudent one does not do simply as others do—he looks well to his own ways; the foolish one passes on with the crowd, and is caught, and then it is too late to mend.

IV. The foolish one loves the bait, and will have it, let the consequences be what they may. He sees when too late. A wise one counts the cost.

V. The foolish one thinks, just as these mice thought, that the one who is taking some of Satan's bait is having a splendid time, and he does not know that the other is caught, and he goes right on and is caught too.

Remember: All is not gold that glitters; sin is not so pleasant as Satan would have you believe.

XLIV.

The Footstool of His Feet.

The Lord said unto my Lord, Sit thou at my right hand, until I make thine enemies thy footstool. Ps. 110: 1.

[An ordinary footstool or hassock.]

I. Jehovah said to my Lord—my Saviour—at the close of His life on earth: 1. Come away from the shame, the toil and suffering. How much of each He had endured! 2. "Come to my throne; come to repose, and honors." So we see Him ascending to His Father. There He sits now.

II. "Until I make thine enemies thy footstool."

1. Even Jesus has enemies. He had them before He came down to earth, He had them all the while He was here, and He has them still.

2. These enemies are Satan, the fallen angels, and every man, woman, or child who refuses to obey and love Him. It makes no difference what the excuse is, every one is His enemy who does not love and obey Him.

Some love themselves and their own ways better than they love Him and His ways, just as Satan and all the fallen angels did; and so they are His enemies; some love money; some love pleasures of sin; some love many things better than they love Jesus, and they make them an excuse for not loving and obeying Him. Every such a person is an enemy to Jesus.

3. They trample His good name under their feet by dishonoring it; they trample His wishes under their feet by not performing them; they trample His love under their feet by not responding to it; they trample His blood—His agonizing death on the cross—under their feet by ignoring it.

4. But all this will be reversed. As I sit and put my feet on this footstool, so Jesus sits and will soon put His enemies all under His feet. As kings in olden times used to sit upon their thrones, and put their feet upon the necks of their subdued enemies, so Jesus shall subdue all His enemies who will not obey Him otherwise. *a.* He is "expecting" it—so it shall be surely done. *b.* He sits while it is being done—showing the ease with which it will be accomplished. Those making great efforts in subduing their enemies are on their feet. *c.* Those who choose not to sit with Him on His throne will have to be under His feet as a

footstool. He died to lift you up, to make you like Himself, and so to let you share all His honors forever. You have to choose between bearing the honor of all His glory or else bearing the disgrace of being a subdued enemy, both of which are forever. There is a great difference between being a prince on the throne beside the king, and being a subdued enemy under the foot of the king. Which will you be? Jesus is now sitting on His throne waiting for you to decide.

XLV.

THE NAILS THAT FAIL, AND THE NAIL THAT HOLDS.

"*And I will fasten him as a nail in a sure place; and he shall be for a glorious throne to his father's house. And they shall hang upon him all the glory of his father's house, the offspring and issue.*" — Isa. 22: 23, 24.

[OBJECTS.—A slender standard, decayed or split at the top. — Drive a large nail into this. Below this nail drive, into the solid part of the rod, a nail which is nearly broken off. Suspend a glass globe upon these, having the word "All" attached to it. The weight of the globe can be sustained by a string running over the top of the rod, and held in the hand till it is needed to have its weight come upon the nails. When this is done, the nails give way and the globe falls with a crash. A large spike is driven into the top of a heavy cross. Have three large boxes with the words "Trials," "Sins," "Soul" printed upon them. Hang them one after another upon the spike as you speak of our trials, our sins, and our soul. A little cotton cord, with a large copper wire twisted around it, runs from the spike down to each box. The weight of these is firmly held.]

Nails are often driven into the wall to hang things upon. If the wall be sound, the nail strong and well driven in, and the load not too great, then all will be well; otherwise all will be ill.

In the picture the small, slender rod has a nail driven into the top. On this is suspended, by a string, the glass globe having the word "All" on it. It hangs well for a moment, but soon the weak nail gives way and the poor globe is shattered into small fragments. This represents the life of very many persons. They suspend all upon some frail little nail or some great nail driven into a rotten substance, and everything falls with an awful crash. A man on the exchange thinks he knows what the market will be. If he be sure, he can make a fortune. He hangs all on the one nail—his judgment of the market. It proves too weak, and He goes down. Just what he did with his money many people do with their souls—they hang their all on some weak nail. It may be man's patronage and power. Cardinal Wolsey tried this nail, and it failed. It may be money, it may be public opinion or worldly pleasure. Sometimes the soul's welfare is made to hang upon the resolve to be better at some future time. All these nails are poor weak ones, and are sure to give way, and the "All" which is suspended upon them will go down into certain ruin.

The text tells of a nail that is fastened in a sure place. It is Christ who is God's nail. It is not Christ as Creator or Brother, but Christ on the cross. That is the sure place in which He is fastened. Jesus the Saviour of man is the nail which is a safe support. This is represented by the large spike driven into the solid wood of the cross under the letters I. H. S. On Christ we can come and hang all.

I. First of all, our trials, which are represented by the lowest large box. Are you homeless or friendless? Hang these trials on Jesus. Are you maliciously persecuted? Have you been bereaved of some loved one? Are you sorely tempted, or sick and poor? Are you exhausted and discouraged by hard work? Come with your trials, whatever they may be, and hang them all upon this Nail. He can carry all, and will never fail you.

II. Do not forget to bring your sins here. Your past sins. Those profane words, the falsehood told long ago, that dishonest transaction, the hatred cherished in the heart against some one, the slanderous report you once circulated, the sudden temptation yielded to which wrought ruin on another, the evil thoughts, acts, and words—bring them all and hang them upon Christ crucified. If they, or any one of them, remain upon you, they will sink you lower than the grave.

III. Your immortal soul needs some sure support, and here it is. There is no other nail in this universe that can safely support your soul. Some hang all on their good moral life; others on some good person—it may be a minister or a priest; others on their knowledge of the Word of God; and others still, on the prayers of Christians. All these are poor supports for the soul, and are sure to fall sooner or later. Christ crucified is the one and only safe place.

IV. But you say, "I do come and hang all my trials, my sins, and my soul upon Christ, but I am so weak, how shall I be able to hold on to Him?" Do you see that cord which runs from those large boxes up to the spike under the I. H. S.? That little cotton cord is your strength by which you hold on to Christ. But if you were able to see it, you could behold a large copper wire running from the spike round and round that little cord down to the boxes. That is God's strength by which He holds on to your trials, your sins, and your soul. His strength is made perfect when united with your weakness. Never fear. Come and hang all upon Christ. He will not fail you.

Now, look at these boxes hanging here. They have no other support. They are depending entirely upon that nail. Make Christ your only support. He alone is able to bear your burdens, pardon your sins, and save your soul. Trust neither others nor yourself.

See their rest. They have not a struggle. The life of the Christian is a life of rest and growth, and not of struggles. The lily grows, but does not make a big fuss over it. It simply remains quietly in the sunshine, dew, and soil, and grows. So you are to rest all upon Christ, and, remaining there, to grow without a struggle.

XLVI.

Simple Objects which May Be Used as Illustrations in the Sunday-school, and in Children's Meetings.

Grass illustrates the brevity of life. Its growth from spring to summer, autumn, and winter, when it dies, is like our growth from childhood to youth, manhood, and old age, when we must die. Most grass is cut down before the fall comes. Most of us never reach old age. Grass also illustrates the weakness of the "flesh." Even the best thing about the fleshy nature, its flower, is so frail that it vanishes when the Spirit breathes upon it. This is the primary teaching of Isa. 40: 6–8 and also of I. Pet. 1: 23–25.

Compasses illustrate the necessity of each one having a fixed centre. While one part of this instrument wanders about in describing circles or measuring figures, the other part remains firmly fixed at the centre. We are compelled to engage in many of the affairs of this world. But one part of our nature should be firmly fixed in Christ as our centre, and then our life will not be an aimless wandering.

Husks, which may be bought at many fruit stands in cities, represent the poor food for which every soul is longing, and upon which he is sure to starve who wanders away from Christ, the Bread of Life. Luke 15: 16.

Pottage, or *Lentils*, which may be had at many grocers', represent the vanities of earth, for which all are tempted to sell their heavenly birthright.

A Flail is often used to thresh out the wheat from the chaff. This illustrates the purpose of tribulations, which Christians often suffer. Tribulation comes from *tribulum*, a threshing-instrument. The farmer does not beat the wheat to ruin it, but to separate it from the chaff. Tribulations do not ruin the Christian; they only separate the wheat from the chaff. John 16: 33.

The Magnet draws all kinds of nails, but not gold or silver; so Christ draws all kinds of sinners, but not the self-righteous. The magnet will draw nails out of sawdust or muddy water, but will draw only the nails. Christ draws sinners out of the worst sins, but He never draws their sins. The nails which touch the magnet have a power imparted unto them that enables them to draw other nails, but it is always toward their magnet. They cannot boast of this power, for it is not theirs. The least separation between them and the magnet breaks their drawing power. The lessons are apparent. John 12: 32; 15: 5.

A Candle unlighted represents the soul of every unconverted person. When it is touched by the flame and lighted, it represents the soul receiving the light of life by the touch of the Holy Spirit (Prov. 20: 27). When a candle is lighted it can light other candles, and is also a guide in the darkness (Matt. 5: 14).

Salt is the symbol of the purity of a Christian's speech (Col. 4: 6). It is also the symbol of a pure life. It denotes perpetuity (Numbers 18:19 and II. Chron. 13: 5). So every one should have salt in himself (Mark 9: 50). Salt saves by its contact. Christians should be the salt of the earth.

Chaff illustrates the worthlessness of the ungodly. When the wheat is taken out of it, it is very light, and not good for food. Place it upon the hand, and a breath will scatter it in all directions. So the breath of God will scatter the ungodly in the day when the wheat and chaff are separated.

Scarlet and *Crimson Wool*, from which the color cannot be extracted without destroying the fibre of the material, represent the penetrating and powerful nature of sin upon our soul. But God's mercy and grace are more penetrating and powerful than our sin, for He so pardons us that, in His sight, we are as pure and holy as though we had never sinned. Isa. 1 : 18.

A Sling, such as David used when he smote Goliath, illustrates the power of little things when used in the service of God and under His direction. Saul's valuable armor could not compete with the little sling which was in the proper hand, and being directed by the right power.

A Sword represents the Word of God. It can cut backward or forward, or it can thrust. It is used to defend and to slay. The Word of God either defends the soul or slays it. It cuts in all directions. When the sword is in skilful hands, it is a dangerous weapon. What power there is in the Word of God when used by the skill of the Holy Spirit! Christians may increase in their skill of the use of this sword.

A Magnifying Lens either causes small objects to appear larger than they really are, or else causes large objects, that are in the distance, to appear larger than they do to the naked eye. We can magnify the Lord by getting a better view of Him in his Word. This requires a long and careful looking. We can magnify Him to others by living a true Christian life before the world. They often see Him only through His children.

A Photograph Plate illustrates the soul of a boy or girl. If the plate is properly exposed to the light, the picture will be good. If the plate be incorrectly exposed the picture will be ruined. So the impressions which are being made upon the soul will either save or ruin it. The developing day is coming. This is the exposing time.

A Rivet holds the blades of the shears together. It may seem very small and unimportant, while the blades seem to do all the work. But what could they do without the little rivet? Love is the little rivet which binds those in homes, churches, and Sunday-schools together, and to God. Zeal, without this rivet, is as useless as the blades of the shears when not held together.

A Leaf from a blind person's Bible illustrates the skill obtained by practice. By continually trying, we become skilful in doing either that which is good or that which is bad. Some are wise to do evil. Some have eyes, but they cannot see God or divine things. Some have no eyes, yet they can see God through their fingers—they can read God's love with one finger. From habit, the blind person comes to have such a delicate touch that he reads readily. So by the habit of prayerfulness and watchfulness the Christian may acquire such a delicate touch of soul that he can know the smallest whisper of the Holy Spirit. So also he can detect the presence of evil, as readily as the presence of electricity is detected by the gold-leaf in an electrometer.

Prince Rupert's Drops illustrate in a striking manner how one under a sufficient internal strain may contain within himself the elements of destruction. They are made by dropping melted glass into water, thus suddenly cooling the glass and putting it under great strain. We are often startled by the sudden fall of a prominent Christian; all such falls indicate that the inward life is formed under a strain; and when the little tip is broken, that relieves the strain, then all the life goes to pieces in a moment. Many characters are being formed under the strain of secret sins. Prince Rupert's drops may be had at nearly all chemists'.

A Toy Boomerang is made of a piece of tough cardboard cut on a parabolic curve, one arm of the boomerang being a little longer than the other, the whole being six or eight inches long. Lay this upon a book slightly inclined, with one end projecting over the edge of the book, and strike it a smart blow with a lead pencil, and it will fly off into the air, but will return to you. Every sin we commit against another is a boomerang which will fall back upon us (Ps. 37:15).

Three Cups of Water, one hot, another cold, and the other lukewarm. If one hand is held in the hot water, and the other in the cold water, and both plunged into the lukewarm water, to one hand the luke warm water will feel hot, while to the other it will feel cold, when in reality it is neither. We cannot judge our spiritual condition or temperature by our feelings. Our surroundings often seem to change our temperature, when in reality they do not. We can test our true spiritual condition only by the Word of God, as the thermometer is the true tester of the temperature of the water.

A Crutch represents many things upon which souls lean for their support. They lean upon their pastor, teachers, friends, parents, money, social standing, and education. The more a crutch is leaned upon, the less easily can it be dispensed with. A crutch is only for the sick or lame. To stand upright on one's feet, and walk, is better. Isa. 41: 10 tells us of the only support we need.

A Compass with its needle always pointing toward the north, illustrates the divine life of the Christian, which always points toward Christ. If the needle is turned away from its north pole, it is always struggling to get back, and is never at rest till pointing in that direction. The needle can be attracted away from its pole only by another needle, which has an opposite magnetism, or by some different metal. A Christian is not drawn away by Christians, but by those who are not, and by things opposed to his spiritual nature.

Mustard Seed illustrate the small beginning of the kingdom of Christ in the heart, which grows more and more, till the whole nature is brought into subjection to the divine life. The mustard seed put into the soil does not always remain the small seed. Neither should the life and experience of the Christian remain small, like the seed which was first planted in the heart. It should be a growing life.

A Coin with a government stamp upon it, or a document with a seal stamped upon it, represents the Christian who has God's seal upon him. The seal denotes genuineness, ownership, and security. The one sealed by the Holy Spirit is seen to be a true child of God, and is made secure for the future (II. Cor. 1:22).

Stubble often looks like the real grain, but it has no fruit upon it. Those not bearing fruit for Christ are stubble. Often one can see the hulls of grain at the roots of the stubble. The life which was once there is gone, as it is gone from the heart of many who once had it. As the stubble is the worthless part after the harvest, so all the proud and all that do wickedly will be left as worthless at the harvest gathering by the angels (Mal. 4:1).

Fishing Tackle, such as rods, hooks, lines, bait, and nets, may be used to illustrate the things to be borne in mind by one who would be a fisher of men. A fisherman must have faith that the fish may be caught; he must have courage to brave storms; he must possess knowledge of his craft, patience in his work, a delicate touch of the hand, a love for his work, and a willingness to learn from others. He must use the right kind of bait, not the same for all fish; he must keep himself out of sight, but go where the fish are; he must use craft, study his fish, and draw the net often to see what he has taken.

Plated Spoons represent those whose Christianity is all on the outside. Solid silver spoons, with the ring to them, represent those whose Christianity is in their hearts, and is manifest in all their life.

A Pear decayed at the core, represents a person who appears fair outwardly, but is bad at heart.

Casks or *Boxes* that are empty, when sounded, make a great noise. The full ones do not sound so loud. Souls that are full of the vanity of self may make a great noise, but that is all there is to them. Loud complainers are not necessarily full of grace. Aching teeth make a great fuss, and "broken bones complain the most." You can usually tell by the sound whether one is full of Christ or of something else.

Plate Glass is composed of sand, soda, lime, and potash. All these, by being put into the furnace and melted, and then rolled under steel rollers, and polished, make the beautiful glass.

So the greatest sinners may become jewels in the Saviour's crown of glory. To become such, they are not to be conformed to this world, but transformed by the Holy Spirit's melting and polishing power (Rom. 12:2).

A Belt represents the truth with which our soul must be girded in running the Christian race. The truth concerning our sinfulness, and

Christ's perfect and completed redemption, is the belt.

The Hammer represents God's Word, which either breaks hard hearts, as rocks are broken, or else moulds them as the hammer does the gold into the delicate gold-leaf.

The Square represents the Word of God by which we must shape our lives in order to have them approved by the great Architect.

Balances, or scales, represent the exact justice of God, Who weighs both the spirit and actions of all. All souls have been weighed by Him, and found wanting. Christ has come,  that all our sin might be cast into the sea of forgetfulness, and we weighed in Him as our representative and substitute. Those balances will not swerve a hair's breadth; and so it must be none of self and all of Him, if we would stand the test.

The Plumb Line represents the exact judgments of God upon our life and deeds. No tottering or leaning building will go undetected when that line is laid against it.

A Jack-plane and Smoothing-plane represent the Word of God as used by the Holy Spirit in the work of sanctification. At first there is much roughness, and the jack-plane takes off large portions of the exterior. Then the smoothing-plane follows, and takes a little shaving here and there, and the result is a smooth and polished surface. After the Holy Spirit's final stroke, the soul is ready for Heaven.

A Cotton string represents my strength, which is very weak. The same string, with a large copper wire twisted around it, represents my weakness twisted into Jehovah's strength.

String and strength come from the same word. The strength of a string lies in the close contact of the fibres, produced by twisting. The soul that is twisted into close contact with Christ has His divine strength.

www.ingramcontent.com/pod-product-compliance
Lightning Source LLC
Chambersburg PA
CBHW032222230426
43666CB00033B/748